A BOOK OF JOYOUS HOPE AND PROMISE

Here is a simple but powerful story that will affect your thoughts and actions long after the final sentence has touched your heart.

YOU WILL NEVER FORGET:

* The four simple rules that can help you perform a miracle in your life.

* The glass geranium that will break your heart.

* The dingy parking lot where Mandino's life, and yours, begins again.

* The ragpicker who rescues humans after they quit on themselves.

* The secret of regaining the self-esteem you have lost.

THE GREATEST MIRACLE IN THE WORLD

Bantam Books by Og Mandino

ABOUT THE AUTHOR

OG MANDINO is the most widely read inspirational and self-help author in the world today. His fourteen books have sold more than twenty-five million copies in eighteen languages. Thousands of people from all walks of life have openly credited Og Mandino with turning their lives around and for the miracle they have found in his words. His books of wisdom, inspiration, and love include *A Better Way to Live; The Choice; The Christ Commission; The Gift of Acabar; The Greatest Miracle in the World; The Greatest Salesman in the World; The Greatest Salesman in the World, Part II: The End of the Story; The Greatest Secret in the World; The Greatest Success in the World; Mission: Success!; Og Mandino's University of Success; and The Return of the Ragpicker.*

THE GREATEST MIRACLE IN THE WORLD

Og Mandino

BANTAM BOOKS

NEW YORK · TORONTO · LONDON · SYDNEY · AUCKLAND

This edition contains the complete text of the original hardcover edition.
NOT ONE WORD HAS BEEN OMITTED.

THE GREATEST MIRACLE IN THE WORLD
A Bantam Book / published by arrangement with Frederick Fell Publishers, Inc.

PUBLISHING HISTORY
Frederick Fell edition published June 1975
Bantam edition / September 1977

All rights reserved.
Copyright © 1975 by Og Mandino.
No part of this book may be reproduced or transmitted in any form or by any means, electronic or mechanical, including photocopying, recording, or by any information storage and retrieval system, without permission in writing from the publisher.
For information address: Frederick Fell Publishers, Inc.,
Compact Books Inc , 2500 Hollywood Blvd.,
Suite 302, Hollywood, FL 33020.

If you purchased this book without a cover you should be aware that this book is stolen property. It was reported as "unsold and destroyed" to the publisher and neither the author nor the publisher has received any payment for this "stripped book."

ISBN 0-553-27972-6

Published simultaneously in the United States and Canada

Bantam Books are published by Bantam Books. a division of Bantam Doubleday Dell Publishing Group, Inc Its trademark, consisting of the words ''Bantam Books'' and the portrayal of a rooster. is Registered in U.S. Patent and Trademark Office and in other countries Marca Registrada. Bantam Books. 1540 Broadway, New York, New York 10036.

PRINTED IN THE UNITED STATES OF AMERICA

OPM   67 66 65 64 63 62 61 60 59 58

"Also I heard the voice of the Lord saying, Whom shall I send, and who will go for us? Then said I, Here am I; send me."

Isaiah 6:8

"Now go, write it before them in a table and note it in a book, that it may be for the time to come for ever and ever."

Isaiah 30:8

To that beautiful redhead
whom I have missed for many,
many years . . .
my mother, Margaret.

APPRECIATIONS

✵✵✵✵✵✵✵✵✵✵✵✵✵✵✵✵✵✵✵✵✵✵✵✵✵✵✵✵✵✵✵✵✵✵✵✵✵

"I am delighted with Og Mandino's latest book, THE GREATEST MIRACLE IN THE WORLD. Here again, one of the greatest inspirational writers of our time has produced a work that will lift the mind and heart of every reader with powerful motivational appeal.

"For many years I have eagerly read everything Og Mandino has written, always to my profit, and I personally owe him a great debt of gratitude. This sentiment, I am sure, will be echoed by his wide circle of readers.

"This new book, THE GREATEST MIRACLE IN THE WORLD, will produce miracles in the lives of thousands of people."

Norman Vincent Peale

★　　★　　★

Today when we face what is probably the greatest challenge history has ever known, Og Mandino's new book THE GREATEST MIRACLE IN THE WORLD should be read by every salesman and sales manager in the country.

Today when millions of people are troubled, uncertain, and confused, Frederick Fell has the answer to all the readers of THE GREATEST SALESMAN IN THE WORLD.

The rich deposits of inspiration left by preceding generations take on a new vital significance. There never was a time when millions of people were more desperately in need of faith, hope and courage and peace of mind, of standards and ideals by which to live and above all an abiding belief in the future and in the progress of mankind.

Lester J. Bradshaw, Jr.
President
Bradshaw Associates, Inc.

☆   ☆   ☆

Og Mandino has done it again! THE GREATEST MIRACLE IN THE WORLD is a fascinating story told in Mandino's pleasing and unique style.

P. H. Glatfelter III
Chairman and President
P. H. Glatfelter Company

☆   ☆   ☆

Whether or not one has read the author's previous masterpiece, "The Greatest Salesman in the World," he or she has an indescribable treat in store in Og Mandino's latest creation of genius. You cannot help being awed by the vicarious influence of the present day Simon Potter, mystic ragpicker who so mysteriously touched the life of the author—and, for that matter, the lives of everyone who reads "The Greatest Miracle in the World."

Paul J. Meyer
President
Success Motivation Institute

☆ ☆ ☆

A SUPER book that will kindle the pilot light of all those who desire to become professional ragpickers as well as those who need to be picked up from the rag-pile of life.

Rick Forzano
Head Coach, Detroit Lions

☆ ☆ ☆

It's Spring again. Og Mandino is back. As we cattle-men say, "he wintered real good."

He returns from hibernation with another novel means of inspiring each of us to be something more than we are.

Paul Harvey
Paul Harvey News
American Broadcasting Company

☆ ☆ ☆

I think THE GREATEST MIRACLE IN THE WORLD has a chance for very wide sales and a chance to be a staple stock item in many book stores for a long time to come. It has the opportunity to appeal to a broad segment of the reading public.

Gerald N. Battle, Manager
Retail Stores Marketing Department
Cokesbury Book Stores

The GREATEST MIRACLE IN THE WORLD is a canvas of colorful imagination brilliantly painted by a master weaver of words. . . . a reading experience that remains indelible.

> Buddy Kaye
> Lyricist—Academy of Motion Pictures
> (Music Branch)

☆   ☆   ☆

Og Mandino has done it again! He has written another book which will rival his classic bestseller, THE GREATEST SALESMAN IN THE WORLD.

> Harlan Smith
> Assistant Vice President
> Kroch's and Brentano's, Inc.

☆   ☆   ☆

THE GREATEST MIRACLE IN THE WORLD is one of the most beautiful and most moving pieces of writing that I have ever had the privilege to read—and to publish.

> Frederick V. Fell
> Publisher

☆   ☆   ☆

THE
GREATEST
MIRACLE
IN
THE WORLD

CHAPTER ONE

The first time I saw him?

He was feeding pigeons.

By itself, this simple act of charity is not an unusual sight. One can find old people, who themselves look as if they could use a good meal, dropping crumbs for birds on the wharves of San Francisco, the Common in Boston, the sidewalks of Time Square, and points of interest in every city.

But this old man was doing it at the peak of a brutal snow storm that, according to the "all-news" station on my car radio, had already dumped a record-breaking twenty-six inches of white misery on Chicago and suburbs.

With rear wheels spinning, I had finally inched my car up the slight sidewalk incline to the gate of the self-park lot, a block behind my office, when I first noticed him. He was standing in the ebb of a monstrous snow drift, oblivious of the elements, rhythmically removing what appeared to be bread crumbs from a brown paper bag and dropping them carefully into a cluster of birds that swirled and swooped around the folds of his nearly ankle-length army-style overcoat.

I watched him through the metronomic sweeps of my hissing windshield wipers as I rested my chin on the steering wheel, trying to generate sufficient will power to open my car door, step out into the blizzard, and walk to the gate release box. He reminded me of those Saint Francis garden statues that one sees in plant and shrubbery stores. Snow almost completely covered his shoulder-length hair and had sprinkled itself through his beard. Flakes had even attached themselves to his heavy eyebrows, further accenting his dark high-cheek-boned features. Around his neck hung a leather cord and attached to it was a wooden cross which swayed from side to side as he dispensed tiny bits of the staff of life. Tied to his left wrist was a piece of clothesline which led down to where it was wrapped around the neck of an old multicolored basset hound whose ears dragged deeply into the accumulation of whiteness that had been falling since yesterday afternoon. As I watched the old man, his face broke into a smile and he began talking to the birds. I shook my head in silent sympathy and reached for the door handle.

The twenty-six-mile trip from home to office had consumed more than three hours, half a tank of gas, and nearly all of my patience. My faithful 240-Z, its transmission whining a constant and monotonous complaint in low gear, had run a broken-field course past countless stalled trucks and cars along Willow Road, down Edens Expressway, along Touhy Avenue, across Ridge, east on Devon and past the Broadway intersection to the parking lot on Winthrop Street.

It had been insanity on my part to even make the attempt to get to work that morning. But for the previous three weeks I had been touring the United States promoting my book, *The Greatest Salesman In The World,* and after I had told forty-nine radio and television audiences, plus more than two dozen newspaper reporters, that perseverance was one of the most important secrets of success, I didn't dare let myself be defeated even by that angry witch Mother Nature.

Furthermore, there was a board of directors meeting scheduled for the coming Friday. As Success Unlimited Magazine's president, I needed this Monday, and every other day this week, to review our past year's performance and next year's projections with each department head. I wanted to be prepared, as I always had been, for any unexpected questions that might be tossed my way once I was on my feet at the head of that long boardroom table.

The parking lot, situated as it was in the midst of a decaying neighborhood, changed its character twice each twenty-four hours. During the evening and nighttime hours it was occupied by vehicles that would have been sold for junk by any self-respecting used-car dealer. These were the cars owned by local apartment dwellers who had been unable to find a parking spot on the narrow street that bisected their soot-streaked buildings. Then, each morning, they all departed in a mass exodus to local and suburban factories and the lot replenished itself with a collection of Mercedes, Cadillacs, Corvettes, and BMW's as attorneys, doctors, and the Loyola University students came into the city from the suburban world to do their thing.

At any other time of the year the lot was a scabby blemish, a back-of-the-hand slap to every resident of the area. In all the years I had parked there I had yet to see its downtown owners make any attempt to remove the litter, soggy newspapers, tin cans and empty wine bottles that accumulated in their own little mountains of disease against the rusty chain link fencing. The only thing the lot had going for it was that there was no other available public parking for ten blocks.

Today, however, with all the lot's sins buried under nearly three feet of snow, it reminded me of a stretch of California's Pacific Grove beach, even to its white mounds which only yesterday had been automobiles. Apparently there had been no exits by the locals this morning. They had probably taken one

look at their buried machines, now igloos, and either
bussed it or gone back to bed.

Entrance to the parking lot was through two posts,
buried in concrete, set approximately nine feet apart,
upon which rested a large hollow-iron-bar gate. To
raise the gate, to get into the lot and park, you de-
posited two quarters in the slot of a chipped white
metal box, waited for the gate to rise after it was
tripped electronically by the coins, and then drove
through. Then the car wheels depressed some sort of
mechanism in the asphalt, automatically lowering the
gate behind you. To leave the lot you needed two
more quarters to bail yourself out . . . unless you had
a special key which you could rent for twenty dollars
a month. Keys were inserted into a special yellow
box to activate the gate, both entering and leaving.

After turning my attention from the bird-feeding
Samaritan, I found my gate-key in the glove com-
partment, pushed against the accumulated snow
which was considerably higher than the bottom of
my car door, and stepped gingerly outside. Immediately I became aware of the incompetency of a grown
man dumb enough to wear low-cut rubbers on a day
like this.

The old man ceased his feeding operation long
enough to glance my way and wave. The dog barked
once and then was silenced by some unintelligible
words from his master. I nodded toward him and
forced a weary smile. My "good morning" sounded
strange and muffled in the noise-deadening snowfall.

His response, in the deepest voice I had ever heard,
seeemd to reverberate off the surrounding buildings.
Once, when Danny Thomas met radio commentator
Paul Harvey, Danny had said, "You had better be God
because you sure sound like Him." This voice made
my friend Paul sound like a timid choir boy.

"I bid you greetings on this beautiful day!"

I had neither the strength nor the desire to dis-
pute his words. I turned my key in the yellow box

until I heard the mechanism activate, then half sliding, half walking, I returned to my car. Behind me, as I had heard it respond for several thousand mornings, the gate creaked as it raised itself for my entrance.

But . . . no sooner was I back in my car, ready to shift into "drive" and ease my way through the deep snow into the lot, then the gate crashed back down to its original horizontal position with a loud metallic clang.

I sighed in frustration, shifted back into "park," reopened the car door, stepped back into the cold snow, slid up to the yellow box, and turned my key again. The gate rose once more, pointed its rusted tip toward the snow-filled heavens, and then fell back. Bong! Impatiently I turned the key again, almost hard enough to snap it this time. Same thing. A short in the wiring, perhaps, from all this moisture? No matter. There was no way I was going to get my car into that parking lot. And if I left it on the street it was certain to be towed away. I just stood there, knee deep in snow, cursing the idiocy of this aborted journey while I rubbed snowflakes out of my eyes.

Just as I was beginning to doubt everything I had ever written or said about the value of perseverance the bird-feeding stranger interrupted my self-pity. "Let me help you."

That voice was truly something and there was a hint of command as well as an offer of aid in the resonant tone. He had moved close to me and I found myself looking up into an amazing face, gaunt, heavily lined, set with large brown eyes. He had to be nearly seven feet tall because I'm no pygmy. I smiled and shrugged my shoulders at this Abraham Lincoln look alike and said, "Thanks, but I don't think there's much we can do."

The deep furrows around his eyes and mouth arched into the warmest and most gentle smile I had ever seen on a human as he gestured toward the recalcitrant gate. "It will not be difficult. Turn your key in the box again. When the gate rises I shall step under it, grasp it with my outstretched hands, and hold it until your car passes through. Then I'll let it fall."

"That's a heavy gate."

His laugh boomed through the lot. "I am old but I am quite strong. And most certainly it is worth our efforts to relieve you of your problem. Carlyle wrote that every noble work seems at first impossible."

"Carlyle?"

"Yes, Carlyle. Thomas. Nineteenth-century English essayist."

I didn't believe this. I was standing in a snow drift with an icy wind lacerating my face, my feet were soaked and freezing, and I was turning into a snowman . . . while a long-haired seventy-year-old hippie was giving me a mini-course in English Lit.

What else could I do? I'm a great believer in considering one's options, but I've also learned there are times and situations when you don't have any. I mumbled my thanks and waited while the old man gently tugged his basset toward the fence, where he removed the rope from his wrist and tied it through two links. Then he returned to my side and nodded. Almost hypnotically I obeyed his silent command and turned my key in the box. Up groaned the gate bar. Then the old man stepped under it and grasped the cold metal bar firmly just as it began its descent.

I'm not too clear about the next several minutes although I've thought about it often. Perhaps the light-and-hurried breakfast and long drive had finally taken their toll. I felt dizzy and my vision seemed to shift out of focus . . . as if someone had smeared vaseline on my reading glasses. Everything seemed diffused. A strange tremor shook my body as I tried to fix on the apparition before me.

Through the falling snow I could see the wooden cross on his chest and perhaps that's what triggered the illusion . . . long hair, beard, hands extended at a

forty-five-degree angle over his head . . . the gate bar
. . . the cross bar . . . the *patibulum* carried by the
condemned man on the way to Golgotha for his
crucifixion . . .

His voice, now touched with urgency, broke
through my fantasy. "Hurry. Drive in! Drive in!"

I scrambled back into my car, shifted into low gear,
gradually applied pressure to the accelerator, the tires
grabbed, and I moved slowly past the stranger, under
the bar and through the gate.

I eased the car gently into a low spot among the
drifts and cut the ignition. My hands were trembling.
My head was throbbing. My legs felt weak. Then I
reached behind my seat, pulled out my attache case,
opened the door, and fell headfirst into the snow. I
arose, brushed myself off, and locked the car.

I turned toward the gate to thank the old man.

My parking lot savior was nowhere in sight.

CHAPTER TWO

I didn't see him again until late spring.

It had been one of those Fridays that never seem to end. Problems concerning routine matters involved with publishing a monthly magazine had increased in velocity and number during the day, and by the time all the brush fires were extinguished I was alone and beat, both physically and mentally.

I sat at my desk listening to the gentle tick of my desk clock and dreading that long drive home in traffic. Even at this hour Edens Expressway would be jammed. Once more those nagging and recurring questions popped into my mind.

"Why are you working so damn hard?"

"Did you think it would be easier once you got to be Number One?"

"Why don't you resign? Your book royalties are already four times larger than your salary."

"What are you trying to prove now that the magazine is a success?"

"Why don't you go somewhere where it's peaceful and quiet and write all those books you've still got burning inside of you?"

Habit, and my own pride, seemed to be the only logical answer to these questions. I had taken Success Unlimited Magazine from a monthly circulation of only 4,000, with three employees, to its present

200,000 and a staff of thirty-four. Yet, I knew there were still 120,000,000 potential subscribers in our country and it was a challenge going after them. Then I tried to remember who had written, "The beginning of pride is in heaven. The continuance of pride is on earth. The end of pride is in hell." No luck. Bad memory.

I tossed my reading glasses into my attache case, grabbed my jacket and topcoat, turned off the lights and locked the office. Except for the street lamp on the corner of Broadway and Devon, it was dark as I walked slowly past the window of Root Photographers, across the alley mouth behind our building, under the overhead train bridge, and through the small opening into the parking lot with its garish and cracked orange-and-yellow sign flashing, "Park Yourself, Only 50¢."

I was halfway across the shadowy lot, now nearly filled with neighborhood cars, before I saw him. His tall silhouette moved silently from behind a parked panel truck, and even in the blackness I recognized him before I saw his dog trailing behind. I turned and walked toward him.

"Good evening."

That basso-profundo voice replied, "I bid you greetings on this most beautiful of evenings, sir."

"I never had the opportunity to thank you for helping me in the snow that day."

"It was nothing. We are all here to help one another."

I reached down to pat the basset, who had been nuzzling at my pant leg then I extended my hand toward the old man. "My name is Mandino . . . Og Mandino."

His giant fingers wrapped themselves around mine. "I am honored to meet you, Mr. Mandino. My name is Simon Potter . . . and this four-legged ally of mine is called Lazarus."

"Lazarus?"

"Yes. He sleeps so much of the time that I never know whether he's dead or alive."

I laughed.

"You will forgive me, Mr. Mandino, but your first name—it is very distinctive. Og, Og . . . how do you spell it?"

"O–G."

"That was your given name?"

I chuckled. "No, my real name is Augustine. Back in high school I wrote a column for our school paper, and one month I signed my piece AUG. After I had written it I decided to be different and spell it phonetically . . . OG. It stuck."

"That is a rare name. There cannot be many Ogs in the world."

"I've been told that one is too many."

"Do you still write?"

"Yes."

"What sort of writing?"

"Books, articles."

"Your books have been published?"

"Yes, five of them."

"That is marvelous. Who would expect to meet an author here among the empty wine bottles?"

"I'm afraid that's where you're liable to meet a lot of authors, Simon."

"Yes. Sad, but true. I, too, write a little . . . but only to pass the time and to satisfy myself."

The old man moved closer as if to study my face. "You look tired, Mister Mandino . . . or rather, I think I shall call you Mister Og."

"I am tired. Long day . . . long week."

"You have far to journey before you reach home?"

"About twenty-six miles."

Simon Potter turned and pointed his long arm toward the drab four-story brown-brick apartment house facing the parking lot. "I live there. On the second floor. Before you begin your long drive come have a glass of sherry with me. It will relax you."

I began to shake my head but, as in the snow that day, I found myself wanting to obey him. I unlocked my car door, tossed in my topcoat and case, closed and locked the door and fell into step behind Lazarus.

We passed through the unswept lobby, past the pock-marked brass mail boxes with their yellowed plastic name-holders, and climbed the worn and pitted concrete stairway. Simon removed a key from his pocket, turned it in the lock of a pine-stained door on which number '21' had been stencilled in red, pushed it open and made a sweeping gesture for me to enter. He flipped the light switch and said, "Forgive my humble retreat. I live alone, except for Lazarus, and housework was never one of my better skills."

His apologies were unnecessary. The tiny living room was immaculate, from the lint-free braided oval rug to the cobwebless ceiling. Almost immediately I spotted the books, hundreds of them, spilling from the two large bookcases and stacked up in neat piles as tall as their owner.

I looked at Simon quizzically. He shrugged his shoulders and warmed the room with his smile, "What else can an old man do but read . . . and think? Please make yourself comfortable and I shall pour our sherry."

When Simon went off to the kitchen I walked over to his books and began reading titles, hoping they would tell me something about this fascinating giant. I cocked my head and ran my eyes along some of the book spines—Will Durant's *Caesar And Christ*, Gibran's *The Prophet*, Plutarch's *Lives Of Great Men*, Fulton's *Physiology Of The Nervous System*, Goldstein's *The Organism*, Eiseley's *The Unexpected Universe*, Cervantes' *Don Quixote*, Aristotle's *Works*, Franklin's *Autobiography*, Menninger's *The Human*

Mind, Kempis' *The Imitation of Christ, The Talmud,*
several Bibles . . .

My host walked toward me holding out my glass
of wine. I took it and placed it gently against his
glass. The rims touched with a soft lovely note in
that silent room. Simon spoke, "To our friendship. May
it be long and filled with good."

"Amen," I replied.

He pointed his glass toward the books. "What do
you think of my library?"

"It's a great collection. I wish I had them. You have
wide interests."

"Not really. They are an accumulation from many
years of pleasant hours in second-hand book stores.
Still they have a common theme which makes each
volume very special."

"Special?"

"Yes. Each in its own way deals with and explains
some aspect of the greatest miracle in the world and
so I call them 'hand of God' books."

"Hand of God?"

"It is difficult for me to put into words . . . yet I am
positive that certain pieces of music, certain works of
art, and certain books and plays were created, not by
the composer, artist, author, or playwright but by
God, and those whom we have acknowledged as the
creators of these works were only the instruments
employed by God to communicate with us. What's
the matter, Mister Og?"

Apparently I had jumped at his words. Only two
weeks earlier, in New York City, Barry Farber, a popular radio host, had used those exact words, 'the hand
of God' when praising my book to his audience during
my appearance on his program.

"You mean you believe that God still communicates
with us as He did during the days of the ancient
Jewish prophets?"

"I am positive. For thousands of years this world
witnessed a countless parade of prophets pronouncing

and explaining the will of God: Elijah, Amos, Moses, Ezekiel, Isaiah, Jeremiah, Samuel, and all the other marvelous messengers until Jesus and Paul. And then . . . no more? I cannot believe that. No matter how many of His prophets were ridiculed, chastised, tortured, and even murdered, I cannot conceive that God finally gave up on us and turned His back on our needs, causing some of us to finally assume that He must be dead since we hadn't heard from Him in so long a time. Instead, I truly believe that He has sent, to every generation, special people, talented people, brilliant people . . . all bearing the same message in one form or another . . . that every human is capable of performing the greatest miracle in the world. And, it is man's most grievous fault that he has not comprehended the message, blinded as he is by the trivia of each succeeding civilization."

"What's this greatest miracle in the world that we can all perform?"

"First, Mister Og, can you define a miracle for me?"

"I think so. It's something that happens contrary to the laws of nature or science . . . a temporary suspension of one of these laws?"

"That is very concise and accurate, Mister Og. Now tell me, do you believe you are capable of performing miracles . . . of suspending any laws of nature or science?"

I laughed nervously and shook my head. The old man rose, picked up a small glass paperweight from the coffee table and held it across to me. "If I release this weight it will fall to the floor, is that not true?"

I nodded.

"What law decrees that it will fall to the floor?"

"The law of gravity?"

"Exactly." Then, without warning, he let the paperweight fall from his hands. Instinctively I reached for it and caught it before it hit the floor.

Simon folded his hands and looked down at me

with a self-satisfied grin. "Do you realize what you have just done, Mister Og?"

"I caught your paperweight."

"More than that. Your action temporarily suspended the law of gravity. By any definition of a miracle you have just performed one. Now what would you judge has been the greatest miracle ever performed on this earth?"

I thought for several minutes. "Probably those cases where the dead have supposedly come back to life."

"I agree, as would a consensus of world opinion I am sure."

"But how does all this connect to those books you've got piled up. Certainly they don't contain any secret methods on how to come back from the dead."

"Ah, but they do, Mister Og. Most humans, in varying degrees, are already dead. In one way or another they have lost their dreams, their ambitions, their desire for a better life. They have surrendered their fight for self-esteem and they have compromised their great potential. They have settled for a life of mediocrity, days of despair and nights of tears. They are no more than living deaths confined to cemeteries of their choice. Yet they need not remain in that state. They can be resurrected from their sorry condition. They can each perform the greatest miracle in the world. They can each come back from the dead . . . and in those books are the simple secrets, techniques, and methods which they can still apply to their own lives to become anything they wish to be and to attain all the true riches of life."

I didn't know what to say or how to respond. I sat, staring at him, until he broke the silence. "Do you accept the possibility of individuals performing such a miracle with their own life, Mister Og?"

"Yes I do."

"Do you ever write about such miracles in your books?"

"Sometimes."

"I would like to read what you have written."

"I'll bring you a copy of my first book."

"There are miracles in it?"

"Yes, many."

"When you wrote it did you feel the hand of God upon you?"

"I don't know, Simon. I don't think so."

"Perhaps I shall be able to tell you after I have read it, Mister Og."

We sat, after that exchange, in a stillness interrupted only by an occasional rumble from a truck or bus bouncing along the ruts of Devon Avenue. I sipped the sherry and felt more relaxed and at peace with the world than I had in many months. Finally I placed my glass on the small polished end table next to my chair and found myself staring at two small photographs, each enclosed in a small bronze frame. One was of a lovely brunette woman and the other of a blond male child in military uniform. I glanced at Simon and he sensed my silent question.

"My wife. My son."

I nodded. His voice, now so soft that I could scarcely hear him, seemed to float across the small room to me. "Both are dead."

I closed my eyes and nodded again. His next words were barely a whisper, "Dachau, nineteen-thirty-nine."

When I opened my eyes the old man had his head bowed and his two giant hands were clenched together, tightly against his forehead. Then, as if embarrassed that he had momentarily exposed his grief to a stranger, he sat up and forced a smile.

I changed the subject. "What do you do, Simon? Do you have a job?"

The old man hesitated for several moments. Then he smiled again, spread his hands in a self-effacing gesture and said, "I am a ragpicker, Mister Og."

"I thought ragpickers disappeared with the soup kitchens and hunger marches of the early nineteen-thirties."

Simon reached across, placed his hand on my shoulder and squeezed it gently. "By definition, Mister Og, a ragpicker is one who picks up rags and other waste materials from the streets and junk heaps to earn a livelihood. I would imagine that sort of ragpicker has almost disappeared from the American scene during these years of nearly full employment, but we could see them again if conditions change."

"I doubt it. Our crime rate seems to be telling us that we've discovered faster and easier ways of laying our hands on a buck—like mugging, armed robbery, and burglary."

"I'm afraid that what you say is true, Mister Og. Still, in this day of soaring prices for paper and metals, I would imagine that a ragpicker or junk man could do quite well for himself. However, I am not that sort of ragpicker. I seek more valuable materials than old newspapers and aluminum beer cans. I search out waste materials of the human kind, people who have been discarded by others, or even themselves, people who still have great potential but have lost their self-esteem and their desire for a better life. When I find them I try to change their lives for the better, give them a new sense of hope and direction, and help them return from their living death . . . which to me is the greatest miracle in the world. And of course the wisdom I have received from my 'hand of God' books has helped me immensely in my —what shall I call it—profession.

"See this wooden cross that I often wear. It was carved by a young man who once was a shipping clerk. I ran into him one night on Wilson Avenue . . . or rather I should say he ran into me. He was intoxicated. I brought him here. After several pots of black coffee, a cold shower, and some food, we talked. He was truly a lost soul, nearly crushed by his inability to properly support his wife and two young children. He had been working at two jobs, more than seventeen hours a day, for almost three years and he had reached the breaking point. He had begun to hide in the bottle when I found him . . . trying not to face his living death and a conscience that was telling him he didn't deserve his wonderful young family. I managed to convince him that his situation was common and far from hopeless and he began to visit me, nearly every day, before he went to his night job. Together we explored and discussed many of the ancient and modern secrets of happiness and success. I imagine I touched on every wise man from Solomon to Emerson to Gibran. And he listened carefully."

"What happened to him?"

"When he had a thousand dollars saved he quit both jobs, packed his family in their old Plymouth, and headed for Arizona. Now they have a tiny roadside stand, just outside of Scottsdale, and he's beginning to command fairly large prices for his wood carvings. Now and then he writes, always thanking me for giving him the courage he needed to change his life. This cross was one of his first carvings. He's now a happy and fulfilled man . . . not any richer, mind you, just happier. You see, Mister Og, most of us build prisons for ourselves and after we occupy them for a period of time we become accustomed to their walls and accept the false premise that we are incarcerated for life. As soon as that belief takes hold of us we abandon hope of ever doing more with our lives and of ever giving our dreams a chance to be fulfilled. We become puppets and begin to suffer living deaths. It may be praiseworthy and noble to sacrifice your life to a cause or a business or the happiness of others, but if you are miserable and unfulfilled in that lifestyle, and know it, then to remain in it is a hypocrisy, a lie, and a rejection of the faith placed in you by your creator."

"Simon, forgive me, but does it ever occur to you

that perhaps you should not interfere in the lives of people or that you have no right to do so? After all, they're not out there looking for you. You must find them and then convince them that they can have a new life if they are willing to try. Aren't you trying to play God?"

The old man's face softened in a look of sympathy and compassion for my apparent lack of perception and understanding. Yet his reply was brief . . . and forgiving.

"Mister Og, I am not playing God. What you will learn, sooner or later, is that God very often plays man. God will do nothing without man and whenever He works a miracle it is always done through man."

He rose as if to bring our visit to an abrupt end, a technique I have used frequently at the office if it was in my best interest to terminate an interview.

I shook his hand as I stepped into the hallway. "Thanks for the hospitality and the sherry."

"It was my pleasure, Mister Og. And please bring me a copy of your book when you have a chance."

During that long drive home, one question continued to intrude itself into my thoughts.

If that wise old ragpicker specialized in rescuing human refuse why was he wasting his time on me, an affluent and successful company president in the fifty-percent tax bracket who had just written a national bestseller?

CHAPTER THREE

xxxxxxxxxxxxxxxxxxxxxxxxxxxxxxxxxxxxxxxxxxxxxxxxx

Several days later, as I was getting out of my car in the parking lot, I heard my name being called with a volume of sound only slightly lower in decibel count than the public address system at Wrigley Field. I looked around but couldn't see him.

"Mister Og, Mister Og ... up here!"

Simon was leaning out of his second-floor apartment window, over a plant-filled window box, waving a small blue watering can to attract my attention.

I waved.

"Mister Og, Mister Og . . . your book, your book. Don't forget your promise."

I nodded.

He pointed inside his apartment. "This evening . . . before you go home?"

I nodded again.

He smiled and shouted, "I'll have your sherry ready."

I threw him a circled thumb and forefinger, locked the car, and headed for the problems of the day.

"Simon Potter, *who* are you?

"Simon Potter, *what* are you?

"Simon Potter, *why* are you?"

Like some simple almost forgotten roundelay from my youth, I found myself silently repeating these three questions in time with my steps as I hurried toward the office.

I had been unable to get a handle on my feelings about the old man and it bothered me. He fascinated me . . . and, for some inexplicable reason, he frightened me. Both his appearance and his demeanor fit all my preconceived notions of how the Biblical prophets and mystics must have looked and acted, and I would think about him at the strangest times, in the middle of a budget meeting, while reading submitted articles, when writing a book review. His face, his voice, his charismatic manner would intrude themselves into whatever I was thinking and momentarily wipe out my concentration. Who was he? Where did he come from? What was this latter-day Isaiah doing in my life? Maybe I'd get some answers this evening. For my own peace of mind I hoped so.

Toward closing time I asked Pat Smith, my secretary, to requisition a copy of my book, *The Greatest Salesman In The World*, from our inventory. She paused in the doorway after placing the book in my hands. "Anything else, Og?"

"No thanks, Pat, see you in the morning. Good night."

"Good night . . . and don't forget to turn off the coffee machine."

"I won't."

"You said that the last time you worked late . . . and ruined two pots."

I heard her lock the outside door while I sat holding the book, my book, my creation that was now being acclaimed by *Publishers Weekly* as "the best-seller that nobody knows." In four years it had never made the big city "bestseller lists" and yet, with a phenomenal sale of four hundred thousand hardcover copies, it had already outsold every hardcover edition of every book written by Harold Robbins, Irving Wallace, or Jacqueline Susann.

Now there were rumors that several paperback houses were interested in acquiring the reprint rights, and they were talking big money . . . six digit money. Homerun! What if it all happened? Could I handle it? Could I cope with all that sudden wealth and the national publicity that would surely follow a promotional campaign conducted by any of the large paperback houses? What kind of a personal price would I end up paying for all this? Would I regret it later? I remembered what Simon had said about the lifetime prisons we build around ourselves. Would this kind of success be a key to release myself . . . or a key to lock myself in? What more did I want from life, anyway? Would I change my lifestyle if I had that kind of financial freedom? Who can really ever have an answer to these questions before the fact?

I tried to put all the "what-if" thoughts out of my mind and opened the book to autograph it for Simon. What could I inscribe on the flyleaf that would be appropriate for this saintlike man? Somehow the proper words were important to me. And what would an expert on Gibran, Plutarch, Plato, Seneca, and Eiseley think of my little book after he had read it? That was important. To me.

I began to write . . .

> *For Simon Potter*
> *God's Finest Ragpicker*
> *With love*
> *Og Mandino*

I remembered to turn off the coffee machine, turned on the burglar alarm, flicked off the lights, locked up, and walked across the shadowy parking lot to his apartment building. I found #21 scrawled in yellow crayon above one of the lobby mail boxes, hit the bell button twice, and climbed the stairs. Simon was waiting for me in the hall.

"You remembered!"

"You reminded me!"

"Ah, yes. Like most old men I am both rude and presumptuous. Forgive me my trespasses, Mister Og. Come in, come in."

While we were still standing we conducted our exchange. I handed him my book and he gave me a glass of sherry. He frowned when he read the title.

"The Greatest Salesman In The World? Very interesting. May I guess who that might be?"

"You'll never guess, Simon. It's not who you think it is."

Then he opened the cover and read my inscription. His face seemed to soften and when he looked at me his big brown eyes were moist. "Thank you. I know I shall enjoy it. But why did you inscribe it in such a manner? Ragpicker, yes . . . but God's Finest?"

I pointed toward his stacks of books. "When I was here, before, you were telling me about your theory that some books were written and guided by the hand of God. I just figured that if you could recognize when a writer had been touched by God's hand you must be a special friend of His."

He studied my face intently, staring at me for interminably uncomfortable minutes until I broke our eye contact.

"And you would like me to read your book and decide whether or not I think it belongs in the same category as the others . . . assisted by the hand of God, as it were?"

"I don't know whether I want you to do that or not, Simon. Maybe subconsciously I do but I hadn't thought about it. All I know, for sure, is that I get the strangest premonitions when I'm with you. You are in my mind a good deal and I don't know why."

The old man leaned his head back on his overstuffed chair and closed his eyes. "A premonition is a forewarning, a foreboding of something about to happen. Is that how you feel when you are with me or when you think about me?"

"I'm not quite sure that explains the sensation."

"Perhaps it is a feeling that we have met before or shared some experience in the past? What do the French call it? Ah yes ... déjà vu."

"That's closer to it. Have you ever had a dream and then when you awoke you tried and tried to remember it and all that remained in your memory were shadows and unrecognizable voices with no meaning and no relationship to your life?"

The old man nodded, "Many times."

"Well, that's how I feel when I'm with you or think about you. I guess the kids would call it 'vibes,' only I can't characterize it because I've never experienced it before."

"The mind is a very strange mechanism, Mister Og."

"Simon, I couldn't even begin to guess how many books and magazine articles I've read about the mind in the past ten years, for possible use in my magazine. Yet, the more I read the more I have come to realize how very little we know about that mystery within us ... or even where it's located."

The old man rubbed his hand across his cheek and said, "Dr. Karl Menninger wrote that the human mind is far more than the brain's little bag of tricks. It is, instead, the entire personality made up of a human's instincts, habits, memories, organs, muscles, and sensations, all going through a constantly changing process."

"I know Dr. Menninger."

"Personally? Really?"

"Yes."

"What kind of a man is he?"

"He's a giant of a man, almost your size, a beautiful man, like you ... and he always has a twinkle in his eyes when he speaks."

"Is there, what do you call it, a 'twinkle,' in my eyes, Mister Og?"

"Sometimes, Simon. Sometimes."

He smiled sadly. "I like, best, what Milton wrote

about the mind. 'The mind is its own place, and in it-self can make a heaven of hell, and a hell of heaven.' Mister Og, our mind is the greatest creation on earth and it can generate the most sublime happiness for its owner—or it can destroy him. Yet, although we have been given the secret of how to control it, for our happiness and benefit, we still function completely ignorant of its potential, like the most stupid of animals."

"The secret of how to control our mind for our benefit ... ?"

Simon pointed toward the book stacks. "It's all there. One has only to study the treasures that lay, exposed, all around us. For countless centuries man compared his mind to a garden. Seneca said that soil, no matter how rich, could not be productive without cultivation and neither could our minds. Sir Joshua Reynolds wrote that our mind was only barren soil, soon exhausted and unproductive unless it was continually fertilized with new ideas. And James Allen, in his monumental classic, *As A Man Thinketh*, wrote that a man's mind was like a garden which may be intelligently cultivated or allowed to run wild, but whether cultivated or neglected, it would produce. If no useful seeds were planted, then an abundance of useless weed-seeds would fall into the land, and the results would be wrong, useless, harmful, and impure plants. In other words, whatever we allow to enter our minds will always bear fruit."

I lit a cigarette and hung on his every word.

"Now, man is comparing his mind to a computer but his conclusions are the same as Seneca's and the o hers. The computer people have a phrase, actually an acronym, 'GIGO' ... 'garbage in, garbage out.' If one puts faulty information into a computer, out will come faulty answers. So it is with our minds ... whether one is thinking in terms of a garden or an IBM Three-Sixty. Put negative material in ... and that's what you'll reap. On the other hand, if you program in, or plant, beautiful, positive, correct thoughts and ideas, that's what you'll harvest. So it's simple, you see. You can actually become whatever you are thinking. As a man thinketh in his heart, so is he. Allen wrote, 'Man is made or unmade by himself; in the armory of thought he forges the weapons by which he destroys himself; he also fashions the tools with which he builds for himself heavenly mansions of joy and strength and peace. By the right choice and true application of thought man ascends to the divine perfection.' Mister Og, note those words, 'by the right choice.' They are the cornerstone of a happy life and perhaps, at some other time, you will let me elaborate."

"In other words, Simon, you're saying that we can program our mind. But how?"

"Very simple. We can do it for ourselves or others will do it for us. Merely by hearing or reading a thought or an affirmation, whether it be truthful or the vilest of lies, over and over, our mind will eventually imprint that thought and it will become a permanent part of our personality, so strong that we will even act on it without consideration or reflection in the future. Hitler, you may recall, did this to an entire country, and 'brainwashing' is a phrase with which we are all too familiar after many sad experiences by our captured troops in the Orient."

"We become what we think?"

"Always!"

This seemed like a good opportunity to do some probing and so I took it. "Simon, tell me about yourself. Do you mind?"

He shook his head, placed the wine glass on the lamp table, folded his hands in his lap, and looked down at them as he spoke. "I do not mind. This opportunity has not come to me in many years, and I also realize that you are hoping I might touch upon some fact, some clue, that will clarify whatever seems to concern you about our relationship. First, I am seventy-eight years old and in good health. I have been in this country since nineteen-forty-six."

"You came here right after the war?"

"Yes."

"What did you do before the war?"

He smiled. "I realize it will require a good deal of blind faith on your part to believe me, but I headed the largest export-import firm in Germany that dealt exclusively with goods from the Middle East. My home was in Frankfort but the firm's main office was in ..."

I interrupted ... "Damascus?"

He glanced at me strangely. "Yes, Mister Og, Damascus."

I rubbed my hand across my face and downed the rest of the sherry. How in the name of God did I know that? For some inexplicable reason I had the sudden urge to get up and run out of his apartment. Instead I just sat there, with two absolutely immobile legs, paralyzed by an unknown dilemma. I didn't want to hear anymore and yet I wanted to hear it all. The reporter in me finally won and I began firing questions at him like some ambitious county prosecutor. He responded to each of my questions at his own pace.

"Simon, did you have any branch offices?"

"Ten, in cities such as Jerusalem, Baghdad, Alexandria, Cairo, Beirut, Aleppo ..."

"Ten?"

"Ten."

"What kind of merchandise did you export and import?"

"Mostly goods with some degree of rarity and value. Finished wools and linens, fine glassware, precious stones, the finest rugs, some leather goods, coated papers ..."

"Your firm, you said, was large?"

"We were the largest of its kind in the world. Our

annual sales volume, even in the midst of the depression, in nineteen-thirty-six, exceeded more than two hundred million dollars in American currency."

"And you were company president?"

Simon cocked his head, shyly. "It is not difficult to be company president when one is sole owner and founder and . . ." he held up my book, pointing to the title, "also the company's top salesman."

My host rose and refilled my glass. I downed half of it as I studied him carefully. Was he putting me on? Finally I grasped his arm and turned him gently toward me so that I was staring directly into his eyes, "Simon, in truth, you have already read my book?"

"Forgive me, Mister Og, but I have never seen a copy of your book until this evening. Why?"

The Greatest Salesman In The World is set in the time of Christ. It tells the story of a young camel boy, Hafid, who had ambitions to become a salesman in order to earn his share of the gold that he saw were the fruits of the efforts of the other salesmen in the caravan. Finally, after many rebuffs, Hafid is given one robe by the caravan master and dispatched to a nearby village, called Bethlehem, to prove that he can sell. Instead, the youth after failing to sell the robe for three humiliating days, presents it to warm a newborn baby sleeping in a manger in a cave. Then he returns to the caravan, believing he had failed as a salesman, never noticing the bright star that followed him. But the caravan master interprets the star as a sign that had been prophesied many years before and he gives our young man ten scrolls of success which the youth eventually applies to his life to become . . . The Greatest Salesman In The World."

"That is a very touching plot, Mister Og."

"There's more, Simon. When the youth, Hafid, becomes wealthy and powerful, he establishes his main warehouse in a certain city. Would you care to guess the city?"

"Damascus?"

"Yes. And in time he opens other warehouses and branches throughout the Middle East. How many, Simon?"

"Ten?"

"Yes, again. And the goods he sold, as described in my book, were the same goods you sold!"

The old man turned his head away from me and spoke very slowly. "Those . . . are . . . exceedingly . . . strange . . . coincidences . . . Mister Og."

I pressed on. "Tell me about your family, Simon."

He hesitated for several minutes before speaking again. "Well, as I have mentioned, my home was in Frankfort. Actually we lived in a suburb, Sachsenhausen, on a lovely estate in sight of the River Main. Yet, my time there was limited. It seemed as if I was always saying goodby to my family at the airport. More and more I came to hate the days and weeks when I was apart from my wife and young son. Finally, in nineteen thirty-five, I decided to do something about my life. I made very careful plans for the future. I decided to work very hard, until-nineteen-forty, and then I would take, from the business, sufficient assets for my family and me to live comfortably for the rest of our lives. Then I would transfer controlling interest in the company to those in my employ who had been so loyal to me through the years . . ."

I interrupted him again . . . and this time my voice broke. "Simon, when you read my book you will learn that my great salesman, Hafid, finally gave his business and most of his wealth to those who had helped him build it."

The old man was frowning and shaking his head at me. "That cannot be! That cannot be!"

"You will read it for yourself. And what of your family?"

"By this time, Hitler had come to power. Yet I, like most business people, had no idea of the monster we had blindly allowed to take control of our country.

My wife was a Jew, and while I was on one of my many trips to Damascus I was visited, one day, by one of Hitler's agents. He calmly notified me that both my wife and son were in what he called protective custody and they would be released to me only upon my signing over, to the National Socialist Party, my entire company and all its assets. I signed without hesitation. Then I immediately flew back to Frankfort and was arrested, by the secret police, at the airport gate. I spent the entire war years being trucked from one concentration camp to another. Not being a Jew, I guess, saved my life."

"And your wife and son?"

"I never saw them again."

I started to say 'I'm sorry', but didn't.

"And your business?"

"Gone. Everything confiscated by the Nazis. After the war I spent nearly four years trying to find any clue concerning my family. Both the American, and British were most cooperative and sympathetic. Finally I learned, through American intelligence, that both my wife and son had been murdered and cremated at Dachau almost immediately after they had been taken captive."

It was tough to continue. I felt like some cruel inquisitor forcing the old man to relive memories that he had long ago probably pushed into the background of his mind in order to maintain his sanity. Still I continued. "How did you get to this country?"

"In my affluent days I had made many fine friends in Washington. One of them interceded with the proper immigration authorities, who waived my lack of passport. Another loaned me money for passage. I had visited Chicago in nineteen-thirty-one and liked its vitality, so I came here."

"What have you been doing all these years?"

He shrugged his shoulders and stared up at the ceiling. "What can an ex-millionaire company president, whose ambitions all died in a gas chamber, do?

I worked at a hundred odd jobs, only to survive . . .
night club janitor, cook, city sanitation work, con-
struction work . . . anything. I knew I had all the
necessary knowledge, experience, and ability to start
a new business of my own, but I had no stomach for
it anymore. There was no reason to succeed or to acquire wealth, and so I made no effort. Finally I
passed the city examinations and became a school
janitor on Foster Avenue. That was very good for
me. I was around laughing children all day. Very
good. And now and then I would see a lad that reminded me of my Eric. It was a fine, decent job. I
retired when I was sixty-five, and the city began paying me a small pension, enough to live . . . and read."

"Whatever made you decide to become what you
call a ragpicker?"

Simon smiled and leaned back in his chair, staring
up at the ceiling again as if trying to remember de-
tails of an event that had been long undisturbed
among his memories.

"I moved into this small apartment soon after I retired. Lazarus, myself, and my books. Each morning
it became a ritual for Lazarus and me to walk completely around this block. One morning, as I was leaving the building, I happened to look across at the gate
to the parking lot, where I first met you, and there
was a young lady who appeared to be in some sort of
difficulty. Her automobile was parked at the approach
to the gate, which was down, and she was angrily
pounding on the metal box which accepts the coins
that activate the gate. I went over to her and asked if
I could be of assistance. She was crying, and between her sobs she told me that she had put her last
two quarters in the coin box and the gate had not
risen. Furthermore she was due in class, at Loyola, in
less than ten minutes, for a final exam. I did what
anyone else would have done. I removed two quarters from my pants pocket, dropped them into the

coin slot, and this time the gate went up. Then I continued my walk with Lazarus."

By now the old man was pacing the room.

"We had not gone very far when I heard footsteps hurrying up behind me and I turned to see the lovely young lady coming toward me, still with tears in her eyes, but smiling. Before I realized what she was doing, she had reached up, thrown her arms around me, pulled me down to her, and kissed me on the cheek . . . the first time a woman had embraced me since my wife. The young lady said nothing . . . there was just the hug and a kiss . . . and then she scampered off. That trivial incident was what gave my life a new meaning and direction, Mister Og. I resolved to stop hiding in my small apartment, to stop feeling sorry for what life had given me, and to begin giving some of myself to others after all the years of self-pity. Actually, you see, it was a selfish decision because the feeling that went through me, when that grateful girl kissed me, was one I had not known for many years. It was the feeling that only comes when one has helped another with no thought of personal gain. I have been a ragpicker ever since."

I felt drained. The questions and answers had exhausted me. Still, there was one thing more I had to know.

"Simon, you mentioned that your son's name was Eric. What was your wife's name?"

"Mister Og, my wife had a name as lovely as her soul . . . Lisha."

All I could do was sigh and whisper, "Simon, please hand me my book."

The old gentleman placed the book in my lap. I turned hurriedly through the first few pages and stopped on page fourteen. "Simon, look! Here . . . where I am pointing, halfway down the page—is the name I gave to the wife of Hafid, the greatest salesman in the world. Read it!"

A half-sob, half-cry of anguish, escaped from the old man's lips as he focused on the printed page. Then he looked up at me, unbelieving, large tears forming in those unforgettable eyes.

"It cannot be, it cannot be!"

He took the book in his giant hands, staring intently at the page. Finally he raised it to his cheek, caressed it gently against his beard, and murmured softly, over and over, "Lisha . . . Lisha . . . Lisha."

CHAPTER FOUR

✵✵✵✵✵✵✵✵✵✵✵✵✵✵✵✵✵✵✵✵✵✵✵✵✵✵✵✵✵✵✵✵✵✵✵

A month passed before I saw him again.

It was well past closing time and I was alone in my office trying to make some dent in the correspondence that had accumulated during my absence. I heard the outer office door click, and stiffened. Whoever had been last out had neglected to lock up, and robberies were becoming a way of life in that neighborhood.

Then Lazarus appeared in my office doorway in a flurry of uncoordinated movements, tail wagging, ears rising and falling, sad eyes weeping, tongue flashing— pulling on the rope which led back to his master.

The old man hugged me. "Mister Og, it is good to see you. Lazarus and I, we were both worried about you."

"I've been away on book business, Simon. I think someone is trying to change my life."

"For the better?"

"I'm not sure. Maybe you'll be able to tell me."

"I knew you weren't here, Mister Og. Each day I would look out my window for your little brown car. No car . . . no Mister Og. And then this morning, there it was. I was so happy. I wanted to see you and yet I didn't want to bother you. It took all day to get up the courage to come here."

"I'm glad you did. I'd have come over to see you, anyway, to tell you the news about the book."

"Good news?"

"I'm still not sure it's happening to me."

The old man nodded and patted my shoulder proudly. Then he led Lazarus to my coat rack and tied a loose knot around its base with the rope. The dog buried his nose in the heavy carpet and closed his eyes.

"You look great, Simon. I've never seen you in a suit and tie before."

My visitor shyly rubbed his long fingers on his wrinkled jacket lapel and shrugged. "I could not come to visit a company president looking like a bum, could I?"

"Why not? I imagine you ragpickers work in all sorts of disguises and have probably infiltrated more walks of life than the CIA. Angels without portfolio."

The beginning of a smile evaporated suddenly when I said "angels." Then he collected himself and forced a wry grin. "Only a writer would coin such a poignant description. Still we ragpickers are very short-handed. There is also a population explosion on humanity's junk piles, and not enough of us to do the job properly. I wonder if your magazine's publisher, W. Clement Stone, is a ragpicker."

We both turned our heads toward a portrait of my boss staring warmly at me from the paneled wall at the right side of my desk. "I think he must be, Simon. He picked me off the junk pile, sixteen years ago, when I was broke, alone, and taking frequent dives into the bottle. Funny, but you ragpickers also seem to have a policy of secrecy about your good deeds. Since I'm so close to him I happen to know about some of the people that Mister Stone has helped and yet very few of his Good Samaritan activities ever get into the papers."

Simon nodded. "That is because we ragpickers all try to follow the Biblical command which Lloyd Douglas popularized in his book *Magnificent Obsession*."

"You mean to do good . . . and shut up."

His booming laugh filled my office. "That's what I mean although I've never heard it put exactly that way. I think I still prefer the original injunction from Jesus, as Matthew wrote it."

"Simon, did you know that when the book *Magnificent Obsession*, was published, Bible sales skyrocketed throughout the world?"

"Why was that, Mister Og?"

"Because everyone began to search for the biblical passage that formed the theme of the book, and Douglas, with a stroke of genius, never specifically pointed it out in the book. Looking for that passage almost became the most popular pastime in this country for a year or more and made *Magnificent Obsession* a bestseller. And those who found the injunction would keep the specific gospel, chapter, and verse to themselves, as if it were a privileged secret that one could only become a part of through one's own discovery."

"We could use that sort of game today, Mister Og."

"Yes we could. Do you know the passage, Simon?"

The old man smiled, rose to his full height, faced me across my desk, cupped his right hand so that only his index finger was pointed toward me . . . and proceeded to send shivers through me.

" 'Take heed that ye do not your alms before men, to be seen of them; otherwise ye have no reward of your Father which is in heaven.

" 'Therefore, when thou doest thine alms, do not sound a trumpet before thee, as the hypocrites do, in the synagogues, and in the streets, that they may have glory of men. Verily I say unto you, they have their reward.

" 'But when thou doest alms, let not thy left hand know what thy right hand doeth; that thine alms may be in secret; and thy Father which seeth in secret, himself shall reward thee openly.' "

I'm positive that it was never delivered better . . .

except on that mountain . . . two thousand years ago.

I poured my friend a cup of terrible coffee and we made small talk as he strolled, cup in hand, slowly around my office. He paused at the wall studded with autographed photographs and read the names aloud, his voice rising gradually in pitch with each additional name, as if to signify that he was impressed. The old fox was teasing me and I loved it.

"Rudy Vallee, Art Linkletter, John F. Kennedy, Charles Percy, Harland Sanders, Joey Bishop, Senator Harold Hughes, Frank Gifford, James Stewart, Robert Cummings, Robert Redford, Barbra Streisand, Ben Hogan, Norman Vincent Peale . . . these are your friends?"

"Some are . . . and the others thought they'd show their gratitude for an article we did on them at one time or another."

"I like James Stewart. All his movies . . . good movies. You know him?"

"I knew him many years ago. I was a bombardier in his B-24 group in World War II."

"He was brave?"

"Very brave. He completed his combat tour long before there was much fighter escort to protect our bombers. And he could outdrink all of us."

"Good. Good."

Simon continued his casual inventory of my office, probably comparing it to his long-ago presidential trappings in Damascus. A faint smell of camphor seeped from his severely cut pinstriped suit and yet he wore it with a dignity and style that made it easy to picture him behind a large mahogany desk, dispensing advice when necessary and also giving hell when someone deserved it.

Finally he put down his coffee cup and said, "I can wait no longer. Tell me of your good news, Mister Og."

"You brought me good luck, Simon, I'm sure of it. There must be a lot of leprechaun beneath that ragpicker facade of yours. Remember that last night, at your place, when we discovered all those amazing coincidences between my book hero and you?"

"How can I ever forget?"

"Well, when I got home there was a message to call my publisher, Frederick Fell. He told me that a large paperback house wanted to meet with him, his vice-president, Charles Nurnberg, and myself on Monday to discuss their possible purchase of the reprint rights to the book. So, that Sunday night I was on my way to New York."

"Were you nervous, worried?"

"Not very much . . . at least not that night. But the next morning, in New York, I was up at six and I smoked a lot and drank a ton of coffee waiting for our one-o'clock meeting. Even so, I arrived at the publisher's building on Fifth Avenue an hour early. So . . . I did something I haven't done for a long, long time. Right next door was a church. I don't even remember its name but it was open and I went in."

"And what did you do?"

"I prayed. I actually walked up to the altar, knelt at the rail, and prayed."

"How did you pray?"

"The only way I know. I didn't ask for anything, just that God would give me the guidance and courage to handle whatever came up. Funny, Simon, but I could almost hear a voice asking, 'Where have you been, Og?' Then, before I knew what was happening, I was bawling . . . and I couldn't stop. Luckily no one was around but I felt like a damned fool anyway."

"Why were you crying? Do you know?"

"I guess being in that church reminded me of all the Sundays I had gone to mass with my mother when I was young. My world almost stopped when she died of a heart attack right after I graduated from high school. She was something special and had me convinced that I was going to be a writer even when I was in grade school. I still remember how she would review my compositions or the other written work I brought home, and we had such a great relationship that she could criticize my work, constructively, and I'd always accept it and resolve to try harder. She was so proud when I became news editor of our high school paper you'd have thought I'd just been tapped by the *New York Times*. She wanted me to go to college, but we were having a tough time just surviving in nineteen-forty. Then she died ... and I joined the Army Air Force."

"You never attended college, Mister Og."

"No."

The old man looked around my office again and shook his head. "Amazing. What else took place in that church?"

"Nothing else. I finally got control of myself, and by then it was nearly time for our appointment, so I left the church, walked across the street and into the publisher's lobby. When I got off the elevator on the twenty-sixth floor I found myself walking down this long hall, flanked by giant posters of some of the most famous writers in the world, published by this firm. All I could think was, 'Mom, we made it. We're here with the best!'"

"And your meeting with the publishing executives?"

"It went sensationally. Large boardroom table, large room, many names, many faces. As we were told later, they had already decided to purchase the paperback rights. What they wanted to learn was whether I was marketable and promotable along with the book."

"Balzac, Dickens, Tolstoy . . . they would have failed that test."

"You're probably right. Anyway, I spoke to them for about ten minutes, told them how the book came to be written, and I guess I made the proper impression."

The old man was now vicariously reliving every

minute of my command performance. He leaned forward excitedly and pointed both hands at me, motioning me to continue.

"Finally, their chairman of the board looked at my publisher, Fred Fell, and asked what we wanted for the paperback rights. Mr. Fell, in his best poker-playing voice replied that he wanted one dollar for every hardcover copy we had sold . . . and we had, at that point, sold three hundred and fifty thousand copies. There was a little gasping and groaning around the table and the chairman said that he hadn't expected to go that high. Then he excused himself, beckoned to one of his vice-presidents, and left the room. I guess they were only gone for a few minutes, Simon, but so help me it seemed like a year. When they came back the chairman went over to Mister Fell, put out his hand and they shook. That was it!"

"It was that simple?"

"Yes."

"They are paying you three hundred and fifty thousand dollars?"

"Yes."

"Mister Og, you are wealthy!"

"Not as wealthy as you think. Mister Fell gets half of that and then we both must share with Uncle Sam."

"But, Mister Og, you have already earned a considerable sum of money in royalties from all those hardcover sales, have you not?"

"Yes."

"Did you know that F. Scott Fitzgerald, three years after *The Great Gatsby* was published, received only five dollars and fifteen cents in royalties and by the time he died that marvelous book was already out of print?"

"No, I didn't know that, Simon. And don't misunderstand. I'm not ungrateful. I can't believe it's happened to me yet. Maybe it was that prayer in church."

"And maybe it was your mother's prayers, my friend. Now where have you been for the rest of the month?"

"Well, since the paperback won't be out until next Spring, Fell decided to promote the hardcover book heavily through this summer and fall and so I agreed to go on a radio, television, and newspaper promotion tour for three weeks. I've been in fourteen cities, been interviewed more than ninety times . . . and I'm getting to like it . . . even the book-store autographing sessions."

"I'm very proud and happy for you, Mister Og."

We sat for awhile, two comrades, sharing a victory. There was more small talk before I finally got up enough courage to ask, "Simon, did you ever get around to reading my book?"

"Of course. The very same night you left it with me. It is a beautiful thing. The paperback people will sell millions of copies. The world needs your book, Mister Og."

That was good enough for me. They could have all the other rave book reviews I had been saving. Simon rose and said, "Come. We must celebrate. One sherry for your good fortune."

I went.

After we were seated in our usual chairs and Simon had poured, he resumed our office conversation. "Mister Og, the haunting similarities between your great salesman and my own life have caused me many sleepless nights. And the probable odds, after all the other coincidences, that Hafid's wife and mine would both be named Lisha must be beyond the ability of any computer to calculate."

"I've tried to put it out of my mind, Simon. I think the extra-sensory perception people call that sort of thing precognition. Or maybe not. I did write the book before I knew about you but you lived those events before I wrote the book. I don't know what they'd call that, but it's still scary as hell to think about. Do you believe it's all just coincidence, chance?"

The old man sighed and shook his head. "Coleridge wrote that chance is but the pseudonym of God for those particular cases which He does not choose to subscribe to openly with His own signature."

"I like that. And if it is one of God's secrets there isn't much we can do about it . . . and so I'm not going to dwell on it. I haven't even discussed it with anyone else. Who'd believe me?"

"It is fortunate that we have each other, Mister Og."

We sipped our sherry in a peaceful stillness that can only be experienced by two people who truly relate to each other, a quiet that neither felt necessary to disturb with words merely to reinforce friendship. I didn't know what Simon was thinking, but I was trying to muster up enough courage to spring a suggestion on him, one that had occurred to me while flying back from my New York meeting with the paperback publishers.

One thing I had learned in New York was that good self-help and inspirational writing was at a premium. Whether it was the state of the nation, or just another publishing cycle, every publishing house, it seemed, was on the lookout for another *Wake Up And Live* or *The Power Of Positive Thinking* or *How To Win Friends and Influence People*. Whenever our country gets down on itself it seems that self-help books rise to the top of the sales charts and most publishers, trying to anticipate the future, were apparently figuring the country was in for another "down." I thought Simon would be a natural. I took the plunge.

"Simon, how many people do you figure you have helped turn their lives around in your role as ragpicker?"

There was no hesitation. "In the past thirteen years . . . one hundred."

"Exactly?"

"Yes."

"How do you know? Have you kept a diary of some sort?"

"No. When I first began this adventure my intentions were good but my methods of trying to help were trial and error . . . mostly error. I'm afraid I did more harm than good to those early cases I discovered, for I brought them partly out of their living death and then, through my ignorance, let them fall back. You see I was trying to deal with each in a different way consistent with the individual personality involved. Only gradually did I come to realize that while we are all different, each unique in his or her own way, our lack of self-esteem which produced our failure is a universal sickness always originating from the complex of either anxiety, guilt, or inferiority . . . the three standard emotional problems recognized by most students of psychiatry. Not being learned in this area I had to be taught the hard way . . . in the gutters and junk piles, and then from my books."

"And when you found this common denominator you did something to standardize your system of assistance?"

"Yes. Man has been trying to solve the challenge of his elusive self-esteem since he first walked upright, and wise men have been writing of the disease and its cure for thousands of years . . . each giving us similar solutions which, of course, we continue to ignore. When this truth became clear to me I spent several months in this apartment with my books, extracting and distilling the true secrets of success and happiness into words that were as simple as the truths they proclaimed . . . so simple that most individuals searching for answers to their problems scarcely would recognize them, much less pay the price to follow such unexotic rules for a happy and meaningful life."

"How many rules are there?"

"Only four . . . and after months of labor and a

mountain of notes, the few pages which contained the essence of the simple secrets of success seemed hardly worthy of all the resarch I had done. Then I reminded myself that it took many tons of rock to produce an ounce of gold. Subsequently I took my findings out into the world and used them in my own manner . . . and they have never failed!"

"You have this material in writing, now?"

"When I had completed my work, in longhand, I brought it to a small printing establishment on Broadway. They typed it, in the format that I requested, and used that master copy to reproduce one hundred sets. Then I numbered each copy, one to a hundred."

"How did you distribute the material? You didn't just hand the thing to every downtrodden soul you met?"

"Oh no. Man usually does not throw himself on the junk pile until after the realization comes to him that no one in the world truly cares about him. When I find someone who needs help I first try to convince him, or her, that there are still two who care: God . . . and me. One in heaven . . . and one on earth."

"Then what?"

"Once I have convinced them that we truly care and wish to help, once I know they have confidence in me, I tell them that I am going to give them a very special document which contains a message from God. I tell them that all I want from them is twenty minutes of their time each day, to read their message from God . . . just before they go to sleep. And this is to continue for one hundred consecutive evenings. In exchange for these few daily minutes, a small price to pay, especially for people where time no longer has much value, they will learn how to pick themselves off the junk pile and perform the greatest miracle in the world. They will resurrect themselves from living deaths, literally, and eventually achieve all the true riches of life that they dreamed about. In other words, the message from God, absorbed day by day into their deep subconscious mind that never sleeps, enables them to become their own ragpicker. Self-help at its best!"

"A message from God. Doesn't that terrify them? Especially since you already look and sound as most of us picture God. Your beard, your figure, your manner, your height, your voice . . ."

"Mister Og, you are already forgetting one fact. I pull these people from their own living hells. They have already deserted this life in their minds. They are positive that they can do nothing to help themselves and so they are willing to grasp at any hand that reaches out to help them. It is a hand of hope."

"Hope?"

"Yes. Do you know that story about the famous perfume manufacturer who at his retirement dinner was asked to explain his secret of success? He reminded his audience that his success had not come because of the fine fragrances or packaging or merchandising methods he had used so brilliantly. He had succeeded because he was the only perfume manufacturer who realized that what he was selling to women was not exotic odors or glamor or sexual magnetism. What he was selling them was . . . hope!"

"That's wonderful. Now, back to this message from God . . ."

"Actually, Mister Og, when I hand the document to them they see that it is not just a message . . . it is a memorandum from God. I had the document typed and printed in the format of a general office memorandum."

I started to laugh. "A memorandum from God? Simon . . . !"

"Why not? Long ago God communicated with us by chiseling ten commandments on two tablets which He delivered to Moses on Mount Sinai. Later, He wrote a warning on the wall of King Belshazzar's palace. How would He communicate with us, today, if He decided to do it in writing? What is the most modern form of written communication?"

"Memorandums?"

"Exactly. They are concise, have a universal form, are practical, and can be found in nearly every country in the world. Our nation runs on memorandums . . . or perhaps despite them. How many workers begin each day with instructions they receive in the form of memorandums from their supervisors . . . memorandums tacked on bulletin boards . . . taped to punch presses . . . at the end of assembly lines . . . throughout the armed forces . . . and passing from desk to desk in millions of offices? A memorandum is most relative to this generation . . . and so what more effective format, in this hurried world, could one give to those who need help than four secrets of happiness and success compressed into a brief memorandum from God?"

His disclosure shook me up so much that I had almost forgotten my reason for bringing the whole thing up. Half to myself I muttered, "A memorandum from God?"

Simon heard me and pointed toward his stacks of books. "Why not? You've heard me expound, enough times, on my theories that God was involved in the writing of so many books. I've merely distilled their essence, eliminated the middle men, and written a consensus message directly from God."

"Dear friend, I'm certainly no expert on such matters but wouldn't many people call that sort of thing blasphemy?"

The old man shook his head in that patronizing way one does when dealing with a child who is obviously having great difficulty trying to grasp what seems so simple to the adult. "Why is it blasphemy? Blasphemy involves dealing with matters of God in a mocking or profane way. What I have done has been consummated with love and respect and with no thought of personal gain. And ... it works!"

"How does it work, Simon? You're not telling me that merely by reading a twenty-minute memorandum, from God or anyone else, that one can change one's life for the better. Can reading anything have much influence on one ... for either good or bad? I remember recently reading some crime-commission report where one of its members had said that there was no direct traceable relationship between pornography and crime and that, so far as he knew, no one had ever yet gotten pregnant or diseased by reading a dirty book."

"Mister Og, the individual who made that remark must be a very stupid and unworldly person. Remember what I told you about the thoughts that a man thinks and how they affect his actions and his life. I agree that reading any twenty-minute message by itself, once, will do little good. But, reading that same message each night, before you go to sleep, opens many hidden passages in your mind ... and throughout the night those ideas seep into all levels of your being. Next day, when you awake, unconsciously you begin to react, almost imperceptibly at first, to the message you imprinted on your brain the previous evening. Slowly, day by day, you change ... as the message transforms itself from words and ideas into action and reaction on your part. It cannot fail, providing you read and imprint each night."

"But Simon, we've had the Ten Commandments for several thousand years and look at the mess this world is in."

"Mister Og, do not blame the Commandments. How many read them? How many know them? Can you, for example, recite all ten?"

I shook my head, and by this time I had almost abandoned my original idea that had triggered this conversation. Still I probed for an opening. "Simon, you mentioned that you have helped one hundred people. You also said that when you printed 'The God Memorandum' you ordered one hundred copies and numbered them. Does that mean you are now out of copies?"

"Yes, except for the master copy, from which the others were reproduced."

"Are you going to have more printed?"

"Mister Og, I am old and my days are numbered on this earth and, as I have already told you, ragpickers are in short supply. It is time that I make the supreme effort to multiply myself so that my work will continue after I am no longer here."

"How, Simon?"

"I would like you to consider a proposition. I would like to see that the master copy of 'The God Memorandum' fulfills what must be its certain fate . . . its pre-ordained destiny."

"How?"

"At the end of your book you have the greatest salesman in the world, now an old man like me, pass on his ten scrolls of success to a very special person. Would it not be fitting if, after all the other mysterious coincidences between your book's hero and myself, we have one more . . . the ultimate coincidence?"

"I'm sorry . . . I don't follow you, Simon."

"If you are willing, if you accept . . . I would like to pass the master copy of 'The God Memorandum' on to a very special person . . . you! If it pleases you, if you become convinced that it can help others as I assure you it can, you have my permission to include it in one of your future books, if you wish, and then it will go out into the world and benefit thousands— perhaps millions— with your following. How better could one old ragpicker ever hope to multiply himself than that?"

Had he read my mind? Or was it just another impossible coincidence that he should offer his writings to me on this day, of all days, when I had been planning to ask about them?

"I don't know what to say, Simon. I'm honored that you would even consider me to be your instrument of transmittal."

"You would be perfect. But make no hasty decision on this. Sleep on my offer for many nights. There is time yet. And of course, if you accept 'The God Memorandum' I must ask a small payment for my work as would any self-respecting author."

"Payment? Okay."

"No, no . . . you do not understand. I am not talking of money. If 'The God Memorandum' passes to you it is necessary, first, that you promise me that you will use it personally, as I have instructed, before you present it to the world. You are a wonderful and sensitive person, Mister Og. Yet there is a look in your eyes that tells me you have not found peace or contentment or fulfillment even with all your success. The world praises you, yet you do not praise yourself. There is that familiar, to me, sense of quiet desperation in your demeanor. Something is undone in you and sooner or later I am fearful that you will explode unless you reshape your world. If you explode they will toss you on the junk pile and this old ragpicker will not be around to save you. That must not happen. An ounce of prevention is still worth a pound of cure. So, when you receive 'The God Memorandum' you must agree that you will first employ it to strengthen and guide you in your own quest for happiness and peace of mind. Then, and only then, are you to pass it on to others who are ready . . . to those who have eyes to see and ears to hear . . . and the desire to help themselves."

"All right, Simon . . . !"

"Mister Og, you have great potential. You are a rare talent. You must not be wasted. I shall see that you are not!"

"Simon, your words make me feel very humble, very small."

"You are far from small, dear friend. Look! Look where I have placed your book."

I turned my head and followed the direction of his open hand toward the tallest pile of "hand of God" books in his living room.

There, on the top of the pile, was mine!

CHAPTER FIVE

✺✺✺✺✺✺✺✺✺✺✺✺✺✺✺✺✺✺✺✺✺✺✺✺✺✺✺✺✺✺✺✺✺✺✺✺✺

"The God Memorandum" was not discussed again during that entire summer and fall while our friendship gradually ripened into a bond of love. Stopping off at Simon's place nearly every evening, and soon during the lunch hour too, were the highlights of my week. Simon's frugal quarters became my oasis of peace and equanimity during each working day, and the weekends seemed tortuously endless away from him. Yet, for reasons I still do not understand, I never discussed him, never even mentioned him to my family or anyone at Success Unlimited.

Simon became my adopted father, my teacher, my business consultant, my comrade, my rabbi, my priest, my minister, my guru . . . my Delphic oracle. I canceled business invitations and skipped social functions to spend my time with him, and I literally began to sit at his feet to listen to him lecture to his classroom of one, me, on any subject.

Displaying an amazing range of knowledge and experience he would expound, for all too seemingly brief periods, on love, politics, religion, literature, psychiatry, nature, and even more exotic matters such as extra-sensory perception, astrology, and even exorcism. Occasionally I would prod him on with a question or statement that was calculated to keep him talking or I might introduce a new subject on which I wanted his opinion. The depth of his knowledge, especially in philosophy and the behavior of man, never ceased to amaze me.

Once he interrupted himself, while deep in a violent condemnation of the attitude of complacency, lack of pride, and standard of mediocrity that he was convinced had become our world's way of life, to ask me if I realized that by listening to him I was taking a "pre-ragpicker" course . . . just as others took "pre-med" or "pre-law." Then he hastened to show his approval of my presence by reminding me that those who eventually became the best ragpickers were individuals like myself, who had done time on junk heaps and walked away from their own cemetery for the living.

For five months I attended the finest university in the country.

Professor Simon Potter taught.

I listened . . . and learned . . . as he skillfully introduced his favorite people to me, both living and dead, through fascinating, little-known anecdotes and quotes to help him dramatize his most pressing theme . . . that we all had more than enough ability to change our lives for the better . . . and that God had never placed any of us in a hole from which we could not grow. And, if we had locked ourselves in a prison of failure and self-pity, we were the only jailers . . . we had the only key to our freedom.

He spoke of our fear to take chances, to venture into unfamiliar enterprises and territories, and how even those few who risked their future in order to advance still found it necessary to constantly fight that compelling urge to flee back to their previous familiar womb of security no matter how bleak their old existence had been. Simon pointed out that Abraham Maslow, one of America's greatest psychologists, had called this the "Jonah" complex, the innate desire to hide from the possibility of failure.

He was a great believer in making decisions and then burning your bridges behind you so that you had

to make good, and he told how Alexander the Great
once handled such a situation. It seems that the great
general was about to lead his army against a powerful
foe whose men greatly outnumbered his own. Because of the odds against them, his army had shown
little enthusiasm for the upcoming battle as they set
sail for what they feared would be their end. When
Alexander finally unloaded his men and equipment
on enemy shores he issued an order for all his ships
to be burned. As their means of retreat slowly sank
in flames behind them Alexander rose to address his
men and said, "see your crafts going up in smoke,
their ashes floating on the sea? That is our assurance
that we shall be victorious for none of us can leave
this despicable land unless we are victorious in battle.
Men, when we go home we are going home in their
ships!"

Simon did not believe that one should continue to
work at a job which made him or her unhappy or miserable. He quoted Faulkner to reinforce his argument,
trying to imitate the great writer's southern drawl:
"One of the saddest things in life is that the only thing
we can do for eight hours a day, day after day, is
work. We can't eat for eight hours a day, nor drink
for eight hours a day, nor make love for eight hours
a day . . . all we can do for eight hours is work.
Which is the reason why man makes himself and
everybody else so miserable and unhappy." Then, to
summarize that particular lecture, he would once
again state his point that a job that made one unhappy should be abandoned. "It is not true, Mister Og,
that a rolling stone gathers no moss. A rolling stone
can gather moss and a good deal more!"

He presented Mark Twain to illustrate his belief
that experience was usually an overrated quality. I
could almost picture old Samuel L. Clemens, in his
wrinkled white suit, saying, "We should be careful to
get out of an experience all the wisdom that is in it
. . . not like the cat that sits down on a hot stove lid.

She will never sit down on a hot stove lid again . . . and that is well . . . but also, she will never sit down on a cold one, anymore."

He had little sympathy for those who blamed their plight or poor fortune on a handicap, either physical or environmental. He reminded me of Milton's blindness, Beethoven's deafness, Roosevelt's polio, Lincoln's poverty. Tchaikovsky's tragic marriage, Isaac Hayes' frightening early years of poverty, Helen Keller's lack of hearing and sight, and even Archie Moore's climb out of the ghetto. He relived for me John Bunyon writing *Pilgrim's Progress* while in prison, Charles Dickens pasting labels on blacking pots, Robert Burns and Ulysses S. Grant fighting the hell of alcoholism, and Benjamin Franklin dropping out of school when he was only ten.

Then I was afloat with Eddie Rickenbacker, who was asked, after he was rescued, what the biggest lesson was that he had learned while drifting about with his buddies in life rafts for twenty-one days when lost in the Pacific during World War II. Rickenbacker had replied, "The biggest lesson I learned was that if you have all the fresh water you want to drink and all the food you want to eat, you ought never to complain about anything."

Simon's point was that no person ever had a defect that was not really a potential benefit rather than an adversity . . . and once he told me a short fable. It seemed that a handsome stag admired his horns and hated his ugly feet. But one day, a hunter came and the stag's ugly feet enabled him to flee to safety. Later, his beautiful horns became caught in the thicket and before he could escape he was shot.

Simon would stare at me and say, "Mister Og, when you begin feeling sorry for yourself, remember the tiny couplet, 'I had the blues . . . because I had no shoes . . . until upon the street, . . . I met a man who had no feet'."

He was always defining abstract words with colorful analogies. Once, when I asked him to describe love he said, "A few years ago, at your Indianapolis race, a fine driver named Al Unser skidded and hit the wall. He lay slumped in his burning car for only a few seconds before another racing vehicle skidded and stopped alongside his wrecked automobile. Then, while the other cars roared past, some coming dangerously close to the second car, out clambered a young man named Gary Bettenhausen, who rushed over to Unser's car and began pulling him from the flames. Mr. Bettenhausen had completely put out of his mind that he was in a race for which he had expended a fortune and months of preparation." That act, to Simon, was what love was all about.

Simon had another favorite in the auto racing world, Stirling Moss. After quoting Thoreau's axiom that men were born to succeed, not fail, the old man would beautifully mimic Moss's precise British accent to make the point that man could accomplish any goal if he were willing to pay the price. He would repeat Moss's famous quote, "I was taught that everything is attainable if you're prepared to give up, to sacrifice, to get it. Whatever you want to do, you can do it, if you want to do it badly enough . . . and I do believe that. I believe that if I wanted to run a mile in four minutes I could do it. I would have to give up everything else in life, but I could run a mile in four minutes. I believe that if a man wanted to walk on water and was prepared to give up everything else in life, he could do that."

And, of course, Simon was always saying that most humans quit too soon in life. "Mister Og, in Sonoma, California, there is a marvelous driving school for aspiring race drivers or anyone who really wants to learn the fine art of driving. It is called the Bob Bondurant School, I believe. Their instructors say that most drivers on our nation's roads abandon their car too soon when they see an accident coming. As the collision looms they stop trying to save either the automobile or themselves by proper steering and braking, when a good deal could have been done up to the moment of impact to lessen the seriousness of the crash. They give up . . . and they pay for it. So do most humans . . . in most of their daily activities."

Then he would rise, scowl at me, extend two fingers upward in a V, and deliver what he said Winston Churchill had claimed was the greatest secret of success ever formulated, and it only was six words long.

"Never, never, never, never give up!"

While his discussions often wandered far afield, they always eventually returned to his concern about the growing lack of self-esteem in man and its usual end-product, a living death. What frustrated him most were the living deaths that finally became actual suicides, lives he had been unable to save because, as he put it, he just "couldn't be everywhere" and there never seemed to be enough ragpickers to go around.

"Mister Og, look at your watch. Fix the time in your mind and then remember this. By this same hour, tomorrow night, more than nine hundred and fifty individuals will try to kill themselves in this country! Think of that! And do you know what? More than one hundred will succeed!"

He would pound the arm of his chair and continue, "That is not all. We will add forty new heroin addicts in the next twenty-four hours. Thirty-seven will die of alcoholism . . . and nearly four thousand unfortunate individuals will have their first mental collapse by this time tomorrow. Then think of the other ways that we show how little we appreciate the amazing creation that we are. In the next twenty-four hours nearly six thousand sick and confused individuals will be arrested for being drunk and disorderly, and more than one hundred and fifty will show how little they value their precious lives by driving too fast, causing their own deaths or the deaths of others. Mister Og, do you know why this condition exists and is growing in tempo, here and throughout the world?"

I would merely shake my head and wait.

"Because all of us know that we can be better than we are. Oh, it is true that most humans cannot translate this hidden feeling into words, but there has been something implanted within each human being that removes him or her, completely, from the animal kingdom. And that something, almost a second conscience, continues to remind us at the most unexpected moments of our dull lives that we are not living up to our potential. It is only logical, therefore, that if we know we can do better and we are not doing better, if we know we can be earning more worldly goods and we are not, if we know we can handle a more difficult and better-paying job and we are not . . . then we do not think very much of this failure who walks around with our name. Gradually we grow to hate that person. Do you know of Maslow, Mister Og?"

"I've never been able to understand too much that he wrote, Simon."

"Maslow is not difficult if you read slowly and think . . . two out-of-style activities in this country, I know. Maslow once wrote that either people do things which are fine and good, and thus respect themselves, or they do contemptible things and feel despicable, worthless, and unlovable. To my way of thinking, Maslow did not go far enough. I believe that most humans feel despicable, worthless, and unlovable without doing contemptible things. Just being sloppy in their work, or not caring about their appearance, or not studying or working a little longer to improve their position in life, or taking that unnecessary drink, or doing a thousand other stupid, small acts that tarnish their already bruised self-image is enough to increase their self-hatred. Most of us not only have a will to die . . . we also have a will to fail!"

Sometimes Simon would even quote one writer quoting another writer. "We are all unhappy, Mister Og. Henry Miller was always haunted by Tolstoy's sentence, 'If you are unhappy . . . and I *know* that you are unhappy.'"

"But Simon, most of us are unhappy only because we have problems. I can take you, right now, to a hospital in this city, where they have ward after ward of tremendously happy people . . . they're laughing all the time . . . they no longer face their problems . . . and there are bars on their windows."

"I am not suggesting an impossible, euphoric state of permanent happiness as a lifetime shield from our problems. That is impossible. Problems, big and small, will be with every one of us so long as we live. Norman Vincent Peale once said that the only time he found people with no problems was when he walked through a cemetery. No, happiness is not a cure-all, it is an antidote . . . something that will enable us to handle and deal with our problems and still maintain our self-esteem so that we do not resign from the human race . . . and the ultimate form of resignation, of course, is suicide."

"Why in the hell do we do such a poor job of dealing with our problems, Simon? Why are we all so unhappy when the ingredients for happiness are all round us? Is that another curse, like original sin, only worse?"

"Why are we unhappy? I will repeat it for you. We are unhappy because we no longer have our self-esteem. We are unhappy because we no longer believe we are a special miracle, a special creation of God. We have become cattle, numbers, punch cards, slaves, ghetto residents all. We look in our mirrors and no longer see the godlike qualities that once were so evident. We have lost faith in ourselves. We have really evolved into the naked apes that Desmond Morris wrote about."

"When did all this happen?"

"I don't know for a certainty, but of course I have a hypothesis. I believe it may have begun with Copernicus."

"Copernicus? The Polish astronomer?"

"Yes. Actually he was a medical man. Astronomy was only a hobby with him. Still, before Copernicus, man actually believed that he lived in the absolute center of God's universe, here on earth, and that all those tiny lights above merely hung there for his pleasure, entertainment, and illumination. Then Copernicus proved that our planet was not the center of anything and that we were just another tiny ball of dirt and stone moving around in space and held captive by an immense globe of fire many times our size. This was a tremendous jolt to our ego. We refused to accept this brilliant man's discoveries for centuries. To pay that price, to acknowledge that we were less than God's special children, was too terrible to contemplate. So, we postponed payment. We refused to listen."

"And then . . . ?"

"Four hundred years later our self-esteem was seriously wounded again. Great Britain produced a brilliant naturalist, Darwin, and he told us that we were not special creatures of God but had our roots in an evolving animal kingdom. He even rubbed salt in our self-esteem by telling us that we were descended from the animal kingdom. This was an exceedingly distasteful pill for man to swallow. In many quarters, as you know, he still has not gulped it down. Still it was a great boon to many, for here was science now recognizing and condoning mankind's bestial behavior. After all, if we were only animals, what could you expect from us? Thus, our self-image, our self-esteem, our self-love, slipped a few more rungs down the ladder to misery and hell. Darwin gave us our animal permits."

"After Darwin, what . . . ?"

"After Darwin? Freud! And more broken windows in the house of self-esteem. Freud told us that we were unable to control many of our actions and thoughts nor could we even understand them since they had originated from very early childhood experiences involving love and hate and repression, now buried deeply within our subconscious mind. That's just what we needed. Now we had a license from one of the world's most brilliant medical authorities to do anything we wished, to ourselves . . . and to others. We no longer needed a rational explanation for our activities. Just act . . . and blame the consequences on our father or our mother."

"Simon, let me be sure if I comprehend what you're saying. Your position is that man, at one time, perhaps through a closer communion with his God, believed that he was truly a marvelous creation, a superior being made in the image of God. Then he began to make discoveries that gradually chipped away at the high opinion he had of himself, until he eventually was thinking, 'If we're not godlike people, if we do not live in the center of God's world, if we are really only animals, and if we cannot control and explain many of our actions, then we are not of any more consequence than the weeds in our garden. If we are not, in truth, very much of anything, then how can we be proud of ourselves? And if we are not proud of what we are, how can we like ourselves? And if we don't like ourselves, who wants to live with that sort of person . . . so . . . let's get rid of ourselves. Let's drive too fast, or drink too much, or eat too much, or purposely foul-up so that we can get ourselves fired from our jobs so that we can sit in the corner and suck our thumbs and tell ourselves that we're worthless anyway, so what the hell.' Is that it?"

"Exactly."

Now it was my turn. "Let me add what may be another nail in the coffin of self-esteem, Simon, when and if it is eventually proven correct. Are you familiar with Professor Edward Dewey and his Foundation for the Study of Cycles at the University of Pittsburg?"

"Yes. Many years ago I purchased a large collection of back-number copies of his foundation's monthly magazine, Cycles. I have them packed away here, somewhere. What of him, Mister Og?"

"Professor Dewey has spent more than forty years of his life studying cycles, rhythmic fluctuations that repeat with regularity in everything from earthquakes to abundance of grain crops to stock market prices to sun spot eruptions, and several hundred other disciplines."

"I know."

"Professor Dewey visited me, three years ago, and said that he had been impressed by my writings in Success Unlimited. He asked if I'd be willing to work with him in writing a book about cycles that the layman could understand. I was so honored by his request that I jumped at the chance. I spent more than a year digging through his files and notes and charts and we finally brought forth a book called *Cycles, Mysterious Forces That Trigger Coming Events*."

"Mister Og, the longer I know you the more you amaze me."

"That's mutual, Simon. Anyway, Professor Dewey believes that there may be another factor affecting our activities and attitudes. He thinks there is a strong possibility that several planetary positions, when they occur, may exert some sort of immeasurable force that effects our actions in groups, so that sometime they make us fight, sometime they make us love, sometime they make us write and paint and compose . . . and all the while we think we are doing these and other things solely for rational reasons. He says that we may all be puppets on a string and that we must learn what controls that string, out there, and then cut it, otherwise we will never reach our full potential nor will we ever regain our self-esteem."

"I like your professor, Mister Og. Now, if you have been raised and educated with these possibilities that you are only a grain of sand with little or no control over your fate, and then you are exposed, each day, to events that drain all your individuality, and you are immersed constantly in the negative garbage that spews upon you from newspapers, radio, television, movies, and the theatre, and combine all that with concern for your personal security, your life's savings, your family's well-being, your own future, and then add to that the fear that the world is becoming a cesspool of pollution or may blow itself up some bright spring day, how can you really maintain any degree of self-esteem when you must spend most of your time and effort merely trying to survive? Why should you think very highly of yourself? How can you be happy? What is there to like in you? What's so great about this life? Who called this heaven on earth?"

"Somehow, old friend, I suspect you're asking me rhetorical questions."

Simon frowned and his shoulders slumped in momentary weariness from his long discourse. Then a full smile transfigured his face, his eyes opened wide, and he raised his voice. "The paradoxical reply, Mister Og, is that despite all the forces arrayed against us we still want, very much, to be proud of our lives. We still desire, with all our heart, to reach our full potential, and it is only because this small flame of hope still burns inside all of us that we weep in shame at our failures, at our gradual descent into the common pit of mediocrity. We are like those figures in so many Renaissance paintings portraying souls condemned to hell and sliding down into the molten fire while their hands still reach out, still reach up, still seek help, help that usually never comes."

"Is there any hope, Simon? Does it really do much good to light one tiny candle in all this darkness?"

"There is always hope. When all hope has gone the world will end. And do not think of only one candle when you seek to overcome the blackness of despair. If everyone lit a candle we could turn the darkest night into the brightest day."

I tried playing the devil's advocate. "But hasn't the

human race been scarred and maimed beyond the point of repair? The world is moving too fast for the average person. He steps off the road, early in life, and forfeits his place to the swift, the unscrupulous, and the mean. For every so-called success story in this world there are a thousand miserable failures and that ratio doesn't seem to change for the better as the population increases."

"Mister Og, I am surprised to hear you talk that way. You seem to be measuring success and failure like everyone else. You cannot mean what you are asking. You could not have written your book believing that success is measured solely by bank balances."

"I don't, Simon. Yet, I can't tell you how many programs I've been on where this kind of question has been asked of me by some interviewer who has not read my book and therefore assumes that I've written another rah, rah book telling the reader how to be successful, which is always equated with how to get rich. Let's face it, 'rich' and 'success' are synonymous in this country."

"I know. It is sad but true."

"Then when you try to explain, while the television camera is staring at you with its little red light shining, that your book has little to do with financial gain and everything to do with peace of mind or happiness, you usually get a sarcastic chuckle and a series of questions fired at you that are damn tough to handle."

"For instance, Mister Og?"

"Okay. It's all very well for you to talk about happiness and peace of mind, they say, but how do you bring a smile to the face of a man who is out of work, with five hungry mouths to feed and nothing in the refrigerator? How do you calm the mind and soul of a young ghetto mother who has been ground up by her environment while she struggles to support her three fatherless children? How do you convince a dying person that he can still enjoy what's remaining of his life? What do you tell a housewife who is certain that she is doomed to a life of dirty dishes and unmade beds?"

"None of those problems you pose are easy, Mister Og, and yet let me remind you, once again, that each of these individuals and everyone else in the world still have their own pilot light burning inside them. It may be very diminished, in some, but this I tell you . . . it never, never goes out! So long as there is a breath of life remaining there is still hope . . . and that's what we ragpickers count on. Just give us a chance and we can provide the fuel that will be ignited by any pilot light, no matter how diminished it may be. A human being, my friend, is an amazing and complex and resilient organism capable of resuscitating itself from its own living death, many times, if it is given the opportunity and shown the way."

"And that's where you ragpickers operate? Among the living dead . . . the losers of humanity?"

"Usually. I have discovered that most individuals are neither willing nor ready to accept help until they have hit bottom. At that point they figure that they have nothing to lose, and so they are far more receptive to my simple technique to help them try to begin a new life . . . to perform the greatest miracle in the world . . . to resurrect themselves from their living death. Do you read Emerson, Mister Og?"

"I haven't read Emerson since my senior year in high school."

"What a shame. Emerson should be read by thirty- and forty- and fifty-year-olds, not teen-agers. Emerson wrote, 'Our strength grows out of our weakness. The indignation which arms itself with secret forces does not awaken until we are pricked and stung and sorely assailed. When man is pushed, tormented, defeated, he has a chance to learn something; he has been put on his wits, on his manhood, he has gained facts, learns his ignorance, is cured of the insanity of conceit, has got moderation and real skill.' "

"But isn't your ultimate goal an impossible dream? Aren't you, like Don Quixote, trying to escape from the reality of this life, and aren't you concerned that you are doomed to the same fate? The old values, the old principles, just don't work today. What you must do in order for them to be meaningful again, is change the entire environment. Simon, you're talking about changing the world. That's been tried again and again. We've got a Who's Who Of Martyrs who have tried and failed."

"They have not failed. While mighty Rome collapsed around him, a wise man named Paulinus continued to care for one small shrine in order to maintain his sanity and equanimity. You can still find his words of wisdom in any library . . . this old and wise ragpicker. Martyrs do not fail when their hearts cease to pump. If they did you and I would not be sitting here discussing the possibility of carrying on their common goal of making this world a better place for all of God's creatures!"

The old man returned to his seat, reached across and placed a hand on my knee.

"Mister Og, why not try to change the world? Why not teach others that they can perform a miracle with their lives? Of what importance is it to man that he does not live in the center of the universe so long as he can create his own beautiful world? Why should man care that he has descended from the animal kingdom once he realizes that he has powers possessed by no other animal? And why should it concern him that some of his actions are triggered by youthful impressions buried in his subconscious mind when he still has the power to control his mind and thus ordain his ultimate destiny? Only man, each in his own way, has the ultimate decision on how his life is lived."

He had said so much that was deep and meaningful that I had to call a halt to our discussion, or at least lighten the mood, in order to have time to digest his remarks. So, I lit a cigarette and tried to bait him. "Simon, the astrologers wouldn't think much of your remarks about man having the ability to control his own destiny."

He nodded his head, sadly, and smiled. "Seers, astrologers, medicine men, palmists, numerologists, psychics . . . each age has many security blankets."

The old man tousled my gray hair. "You know Shakespeare, Mister Og?"

"A little."

" 'The fault, dear Brutus, is not in our stars, but in ourselves . . .' "

CHAPTER SIX

I surprised him with a gift on his seventy-ninth birthday.

The shock that I had remembered the exact date, November thirteen, from one of our very first conversations together almost did the old boy in.

I detest shopping but I had spent two torturous Saturdays searching for something unique and relevant to buy Simon. I finally found it in Marshall Field's at Woodfield . . . an Italian cast-glass geranium plant. It stood nearly two feet tall with coloring and leafing so natural that unless one touched it there was no way to know that it hadn't been grown and pampered in the fussiest of greenhouses.

Simon owned a window box, the only one hanging outside any apartment window on the entire blighted block. He said he had built and hung it soon after he had moved in, and each year he would haul it in and carefully paint it with fresh green paint. Also, each spring, he would plant countless seedling geranium plants, his favorite flower, in that box, and they would always struggle their way skywards, then turn ugly shades of yellow and lavender and finally wither and die. Last year, he told me, he tried to change his luck by waiting until early summer and buying plants already full-grown and in bloom. Two weeks later they were brown and dead. Still he never gave up. He already had a new strain picked out in a seed catalog that he looked forward to trying next spring.

The old man insisted he had never lost a geranium in either his Damascus or his Sachsenhausen gardens. Once he went into a long description of how he would dig his favorite plants before frost came, hang them in his basements to dry, and then replant them in the spring ... one of his earliest successes at helping living things to start new lives, he chuckled. Some of his geraniums had been more than twenty years old. But not in Chicago. Simon blamed it on the pollution.

"How can anything survive in this rain of death from above and from the gasoline monsters on the street? Look outside, Mister Og. It is a full moon, tonight. Can you see it? No! We are engulfed in our own refuse. We bathe in it. We breathe it. We eat it. Even the water that I pour on my plants contains chemicals that would kill a cockroach. Today, only the plants and birds die. Tomorrow, who knows? Still I have faith that eventually I shall grow a geranium and that the human race will awake in time to prevent their world from becoming a giant junk pile."

"It's going to take an army of ragpickers to accomplish that, Simon."

"In order for this planet to survive, each human must eventually become his own ragpicker. He must not depend on his neighbor for salvation. Believe me, Mister Og, this will come to pass."

They had gift-wrapped the glass plant for me at Field's with one of their most extravagant papers, and when he opened the door I placed the large gold box in his hands and just said, "Happy birthday, old friend."

He took the box, mouth open, speechless. Then large tears popped from the corner of each eye and ran down deep wrinkles on both cheeks. He placed the box carefully on the floor and hugged me. Finally he placed one giant hand on each side of my face and kissed me on the forehead.

"Mister Og, this is the first birthday present I have received in thirty-five years. How did you know the day?"

"Oh, you let it slip one night. Open the box."

"I cannot. It is too magnificent to open. The paper, it is so lovely. It should not be torn."

"It's only paper. Go ahead. Open it."

Simon lowered his huge frame onto the rug and drew the large box toward him so that one long leg was on each side of it. First he carefully untied the ribbon and gently removed it. Then he slid his fingers under the paper, wherever he came in contact with sealing tape, and slowly peeled away the wrapping to eventually uncover a large brown cardboard box. Then he took out his pocket knife, cut the glued strip across the top, and moved back the cover flaps. He looked inside and frowned. Then he began to remove the yards of tissue paper which had been packed tightly around the plant, savoring each moment with the kind of childish excitement and anticipation that one usually sees only at Christmas. At last he reached in and tenderly removed his gift of glass from the carton.

"A geranium! I cannot believe it. A pelargonium of the highest class! A show flower, a blue ribbon aristocrat if ever I have seen one. And it's not real. God! It's made of glass! Mister Og, where did you find such an incredible work of art? And look . . . look at the crimson of its blooms! Once, in Jerusalem, I saw a geranium with this same iridescent glow. I tried to purchase it from its owner but did not succeed. Such a gift. Such an expensive gift, Mister Og. What can I say?"

"Don't say anything, Simon. I'm happy that it pleases you. It's only a small token of love and thanks for all the hours of wisdom and hope you have shared with me. Happy birthday . . . and may you have seventy-nine more."

By now he was on his feet, carrying the plant from

place to place, searching for the ideal spot to display it. He set it on the coffee table, stepped back, studied it for several minutes, shook his head and removed it. Then he tried it on top of the television set. No. Then the end table behind the pictures of his family. Better. But still no.

Watching him fuss and move his gift from place to place I suddenly had an inspiration. "Simon, there is really only one perfect spot for that geranium."

He paused, reluctantly, as if I were spoiling his fun. "Where, Mister Og?"

"Well, it's made of glass so the pollution won't hurt it. Why not plant it outside, in your window box? Who else, in this entire city, will have a red geranium in their window box blooming its heart out in November . . . and December . . . and January and every other month of the year?"

"That is a stroke of genius, Mister Og. And it can stand out there to bid you good morning, each day, as you drive into the parking lot. I shall do it. But . . . you must perform the honors."

"Honors? What do you mean?"

"You must plant it for me. Wait . . . wait . . . I'll get my trowel."

And so the two of us planted our ninety-five dollar glass geranium. We wrestled with the ice-stuck living room window until it grudgingly moved upward and, while cold blasts of premature winter winds nearly took my breath away, I leaned out and chipped a hole in the almost frozen black dirt in the window box. Simon handed me the plant and I buried the pot, covering it with sand, so that only the plant showed. Then we stepped back to admire our landscaping as the warm light from the living room reflected off the plant's petals.

"It is beautiful, it is very special," Simon shouted. "Now I have my geranium at last. You see, he who perseveres never fails. Who but you would find such a present!"

"It's for my favorite ragpicker, that's all."

Then we drank a toast, sherry of course, to his seventy-nine years, and as we sat I could see that he was fighting to keep his emotions under control. His lips were quivering slightly and his eyes were half shut. I wondered what memory he was submerged in but I kept still. Finally he shook his head, as if to clear it, and said, "Nothing is more disgraceful than that an old man should have nothing to show to prove that he has lived long, except his years."

"I know who said that. Seneca, right?"

"Mister Og, you are too smart to be only fifty years old."

"But you have much to show for your years, Simon. Just considering only these years you have lived as a ragpicker with all those people you have helped . . ."

"Yes . . . my angels from the dump. I loved each one of them. They are my ticket to heaven . . . my passport to Lisha . . . and Eric."

"Simon, I like Henry Ford's remark about growing old better than Seneca's."

"Yes?"

"Ford said that if you took all the experience and judgment of people over fifty out of the world there wouldn't be enough brains and talent left to run it."

"But, Mister Og, Ford did not say that until after he had passed the age of fifty. And then, of course, there was the saying of that eighteenth-century German humorist, Richter. Do you know it?"

"I knew you'd top me. Go ahead."

"Richter said, 'Like a morning dream, life becomes more and more bright the longer we live, and the reason of everything appears more clear. What has puzzled us before seems less mysterious, and the crooked paths look straighter as we approach the end.'"

As if drawn by some giant magnetic force I suddenly rose from my chair, went over to Simon, and sat at his feet. I looked up into his beautiful face and said, "'The God Memorandum.' I think I'm ready for it. I would consider it an honor and a privilege for you to give it to me and I promise you that I'll do everything in my power to deliver it to the world. I can think of no time in our history when we have needed it more."

The old man sighed softly, a look of almost overwhelming relief on his face. "I was afraid you had rejected my offer or, as the months passed, had even forgotten it. Your acceptance is a greater gift than even my geranium. Still, I have had second thoughts about my offer since I made it to you."

"You mean you've changed your mind, Simon."

"No, no . . . not that. Only concern that people may not take its message seriously, Mister Og, since it is so unsophisticated, brief, and basic. In these days it seems that the more complicated, high-sounding, and expensive one makes self-help instruction, the more people are attracted to it, while they tend to put down those such as Dale Carnegie, Dorothea Brande, Napoleon Hill, Norman Vincent Peale, and even your W. Clement Stone who offer simple but workable solutions to life's problems. Furthermore, it is one thing to advise and counsel an individual, in the flesh, prior to introducing him or her to 'The God Memorandum,' because the power of your personality hopefully adds credence to your gift. It is quite another matter for words on paper, with no preliminary, personal mind-conditioning, to be forceful enough to motivate the reader into action."

"Simon, there will always be a small group of detractors, long on education and short on experience, ready to accuse you of offering pap and simplistic solutions to what they classify as extremely complicated problems, usually requiring five years of therapy at fifty bucks a weekly visit. Yet I would like a dollar for every human who has been inspired and helped, truly helped, by reading Carnegie, Peale,

Brande, Hill, Stone, and many others, without ever meeting the authors."

"Including Mandino."

"I'd join that group any day they'd have me. Simon, do you still want to multiply yourself? Do you still want to help thousands instead of only a handful?"

"Of course."

"Well, there are two ingredients necessary for 'The God Memorandum' to become a success. First, there must be a need for it and then it must have a showcase that will assure its wide distribution to those in need. I remember that Lillian Roth, in her book *I'll Cry Tomorrow*, wrote that she had been unable to rescue herself from her own living death, alcoholism, until she finally learned to say the three most difficult words she ever uttered. Those words were 'I need help.' You told me, yourself, that the best time to help people was when they had lost all hope and had no one left to turn to for support. Simon, if you listen, you can almost hear a chorus of millions from every neighborhood and status and profession in the world, crying for help. The need for your message, right now, is so great that we'll probably never be able to fill it as well as we would like. Rich or poor, black or white, beautiful or ugly, crowded or lonely ... they all need help. There are millions who believe that life, their life, has been not heaven, but hell ... on earth."

Simon had cocked his head and was hanging on my words as I usually hung on his. His made no reply and so I continued.

"The second ingredient to assure success is that the 'Memorandum' have the proper showcase and distribution. I haven't even read it, yet, but I promise you this ... I will make 'The God Memorandum' a part of my next book and I will also write about you ... and I will call the book *The Greatest Miracle In The World*. We'll show the world how to perform that miracle . . . how to recycle their own lives and come back from their living deaths."

"You would do that for me?"

"For you, of course . . . but also for all those human beings who want a chance to live and don't even realize it's still theirs for the taking."

Suddenly his booming laugh filled the apartment. "Mister Og, as I recall from my presidential days, most memorandums have carbon copies going to various individuals or departments within an organization. 'The God Memorandum' . . . should we carbon the world with it?"

"Why not? We've got four billion workers in this company of ours, all struggling for a promotion to a better life . . . or willing to struggle if they knew how. Let's give them all a chance to pull off the greatest miracle in the world and when that happens we'll have our heaven right here!"

"We'll show them how, Mister Og, we'll show them how."

"Simon, as usual when I'm with you I've lost track of the time. I must run. May I take the 'Memorandum' to read over the weekend?"

His almost imperceptible hesitation would have gone unnoticed by anyone else. "Not tonight, my friend, but soon . . . very soon, it will be in your possession."

I knew enough not to push him. "Okay. Good night, old man."

"Good night, young man. And thank you for a birthday party I shall never forget. You have truly lit a candle for me this night."

As I walked under the parking lot gate that he had held up for me in that snowstorm, nearly a year ago, I turned and looked up at his apartment window.

There, silhouetted against the warm light from his living room, swayed the dark outline of Simon's new red geranium.

CHAPTER SEVEN

✾✲✾✲✾✲✾✲✾✲✾✲✾✲✾✲✾✲✾✲✾✲✾✲✾✲✾✲✾✲✾✲✾✲

The thick brown manilla envelope rested ominous-
ly on my desk on that Monday that I shall never forget.

I had been away again on what I had been assured
would be the final promotional tour for my book. This
jaunt had consumed two weeks, twelve flights, ten
cities, ten strange hotel beds, ten early wake-up calls
. . . and the same endless series of questions and answers from New Orleans to Monterey.

I arrived at the office early, hoping to get an hour's
jump on what I expected would be an overflowing
"In" basket. The smell of freshly brewed coffee per-
meated the place. Only Vi Noramzyk, who had been
coming in early forever, had arrived ahead of
me.

I picked up the brown envelope and stared at the
gentle European script on its front with a combination of horror and panic. In the upper left-hand corner, where one normally puts a return address, were
the words:

A farewell gift from an old ragpicker

In the center of the envelope was my name and
my business address.

In the upper right-hand corner stamps had been

affixed . . . one dollar and twenty cents worth. They were uncanceled. There was no postmark.

I dropped the package and dashed out of the office. Just as I threw open the door leading to the hall Pat walked in. Her "welcome back" smile vanished when she saw the look on my face. "What's the matter?"

I grabbed her by her arm and almost pushed her into my office. Then I stooped to pick up the package from where I had dropped it on the carpeting, and held it up. "When did we get this?"

She took the envelope from my hand, read the message, and shrugged her shoulders. "I don't know. All your mail is on the couch. I've never seen that before. It wasn't here when I locked up on Friday. Must have come this morning. By messenger, maybe?"

I jerked the phone off its cradle and punched the digits 24 . . . our subscription department. Barbara Voigt, our subscription manager, didn't even get a chance to welcome me back. "Barbara, please ask Vi to come into my office."

Vi was soon standing uncomfortably in my doorway, her pretty cherublike face registering concern and puzzlement as to why I would want to see her. "Vi, did you open up this morning?"

"Yes, I always do."

"I know. Did anyone deliver this package to you?"

"No."

"Did you see any strangers in the hall when you arrived?"

"No. No one was around except Charlie, the janitor. I just fixed the coffee, like always, waited until the pot filled, poured myself a cup and went back across the hall. Why. What's the matter?"

"That's okay, Vi. Never mind. Thanks."

I tossed the package on my desk, grabbed my topcoat and ran out of the office. The sidewalk was beginning to turn white from Chicago's first winter snow, and I vaguely remember slipping and falling several times as I ran through the parking lot, across Winthrop Street, into Simon's apartment lobby. I didn't bother to hit the bell and leaped up the stairs two at a time. When I reached the second floor landing I turned and began pounding on the door of Simon's apartment.

The door finally flew open and I was staring at a red-faced plump woman, her hair in pin curls, holding a crying infant. Another young and grubby child was clinging tightly to the woman's faded pink nightrobe. Simon must be involved in another ragpicking mission of mercy, I thought.

"Mr. Potter, please."

"Who?"

"Mr. Potter. The old man. He lives here."

"Ain't nobody named Potter here."

"What are you talking about? He's lived here for years. Tell him Og Mandino is here."

"Look, Mac, my name is Johnson. I've lived in this dump for four years and I damn well ought to know there ain't nobody named Potter here."

She began to close the door but I stopped it with my arm and stepped into the apartment. "Come on, lady, don't play games with me. I've been in this apartment a hundred times in the past year. An old man named Simon Potter lives here. Where is he?"

Before she could answer, my eyes swept the apartment, and I could feel the hair rising at the back of my neck. Nothing was familiar. Our two favorite talk chairs were gone. There were no books piled high along the living room wall. The braided rug had been replaced by an ugly, checkered orange-and-blue linoleum. The woman, now clutching her child closer to her breast, growled, "Mac, I'll give you just five seconds to get your ass out of here and then I'm going to start yelling and call the cops. Who the hell do you think you are breaking into my apartment, you creep! You ought to be in jail or a nut house. Get out of here!"

I felt weak in the knees. My stomach was flopping. I wanted to vomit. I backed slowly toward the door and raised my hands, helplessly. "I'm sorry, lady. Maybe I'm in the wrong apartment. Do you know Simon Potter? Old man, dark, very tall, and he has a dog, a bassett?"

"There ain't nobody like that in this building. I ought to know, I been here for four years."

"Next door?"

"That way, a little old Italian lady and her daughter. That way, there, a black man lives all alone. There ain't no guy named Potter here, I tell ya. Now scram!"

I apologized again and stepped out into the hall. The door slammed shut and I was staring at the red painted numerals with which I had become so familiar . . . 21. I still felt weak and so I sat on the stairway trying to collect my thoughts. Where was he? Was I dreaming all this? If so, what a hell of a nightmare I was having.

Any moment, I thought, Rod Serling would walk up the stairs and welcome me to another edition of "Night Gallery."

Then an idea. I ran down the stairs, past the lobby, down another flight to the basement. At the far end I could see a light and hear the drone of the oil furnace. A slight shadowy figure was leaning back in a chair under the single fly-specked light bulb. "Are you the janitor?"

"Yes, sir, yes, sir."

"Been here long?"

"All night."

"No, no . . . I mean have you worked here long?"

"Be eleven years in February."

"Is there a Simon Potter registered as a tenant in

this building? Tall man, dark, long hair. Beard. Looks a lot like Abraham Lincoln. Has a dog, a bassett."

"We don't allow dogs in the building."

"Do you know the man I've described?"

"No, sir."

"Have you ever seen the man I've described, either here or outside on the street?"

"No, sir. I know everyone in the building and nearly everyone in the neighborhood. There ain't no such man here and there ain't been no such man around this block in the past eleven years, I guarantee you that."

"You're sure?"

"I'm positive."

I ran back up the steps, across the street to the parking lot and unlocked my car. Eventually I was at the Foster Avenue Police Station although I still don't remember driving there. I parked my car smack between two blue squad cars and ran into the station. I waited impatiently at the wire window until a young sergeant nodded curtly at me.

"Sergeant, my name is Mandino and I have a business over on Broadway."

"Yes, sir."

"Someone is missing. I had a friend who lived in an apartment at 6353 Winthrop Street. I've known him for more than a year. I've been away from my office for a couple of weeks and when I got back, this morning, there was a package on my desk with my name and address and some words in the upper left-hand corner to the effect that it was a farewell gift from him."

"What was in the package?"

"I don't know. As soon as I read that farewell message bit I ran to his apartment and . . ."

"And?"

"He wasn't there. Furthermore the people who

were in his apartment said that he had never lived there . . . and they didn't know anyone like the man I was describing."

"You sure you had the right apartment?"

"I've been in it a hundred times. Apartment twenty-one. I talked to the janitor of the building. He didn't know anyone by the name of Simon Potter. Said there had never been such a person in the building in the past eleven years that he worked there. No Simon Potter."

"Are you all right, sir?"

"Yes, I'm all right. I'm sober and I'm no nut, honest. How the hell could I make up this kind of a crazy story?"

"We've heard crazier."

"I'll bet you have."

"What was that guy's name again?"

"Potter . . . Simon Potter. Almost eighty years old. Dark long hair. And a beard. Tall. Had a dog . . . a bassett hound."

The sergeant lit a cigarette and studied me closely for several seconds. Then he turned without saying another word and went into the back office. Perhaps fifteen minutes passed before he returned. "We haven't picked up anyone by that name or answering your friend's description in at least the past three weeks in this precinct. But this is a big city. Why don't you try Cook County Hospital?"

"Okay."

"And one other spot."

"Where?"

"The county morgue down on West Polk."

I struck out at the hospital. They were considerate and patient with me and checked back through their records for the past fourteen days. No one with Simon's name or fitting Simon's description had been brought in for any sort of treatment. They also suggested I check with the morgue. I went. There they treated my story casually . . . as if I were someone filing a complaint in a giant department store. They obviously heard similar stories, hourly, about missing fathers, sons, brothers, sisters, lovers. Methodically they checked their microfilm files and one young man finally came forward holding a small clipboard. "Sir, we have one 'unidentified' who fits the age and general description. Want to take a look?"

I nodded and followed him. As we walked along the brightly lit white antiseptic-smelling corridor he touched my arm and said, "Don't let the stench get you. They still haven't invented a deodorant to wipe out these smells."

Finally he pushed open a swinging door and we entered a chilly room with giant drawers sitting in rows like ghoulish file cabinets. He checked the number on his pad and pulled heavily on one of the drawer handles. I turned my head away, not wanting to look. Finally I forced myself and I was staring down at the nude body of a very old man, his long hair wrapped around his face and chest, his eyes still half open. My heart was thumping as I leaned forward to have a better look at this poor unclaimed nameless human who had fallen on his last junk pile.

It wasn't Simon.

Finally I tried Missing Persons on South State. Zero.

The snow was still falling as I pulled up to my parking lot. I got out, turned the key, and watched the gate move slowly toward the sky, remembering again that first day in the snow when a strange, beautiful man came into my life and held up the world in his bare hands for me. I stepped back into the car, punched the steering wheel with my fists, shifted, and slammed the car into a parking place.

I must have looked terrible. My own staff people turned away from me, as if not to notice my presence, when I reentered the office, tracking snow across the red carpet of the reception area. As I passed Pat's desk I nodded toward my office and she rose and followed me.

"Close the door, hon . . . and have a seat."

She frowned and sat facing me. Her eyes were wide with both fear and concern.

"My God, Og, what's the matter?"

"I think I must be going crazy, Pat. Now listen to me. You live on Winthrop Street, don't you?"

"Yes. About a block down."

"Every morning when you walk to work do you cut through the parking lot?"

"Yes."

"Have you ever seen a strange old man around the parking lot. He wears funny old clothes and usually is feeding the pigeons. He has long hair and a beard and he always has a bassett hound with him."

Pat thought for a few moments and shook her head. "There are usually a few winos hanging around the lot, but no one like that."

"You've never seen this man? He's very tall and very old. Sometimes he wears a wooden crucifix around his neck?"

"Never. What's the matter, Og? What's happened?"

"It's okay, hon. I'll tell you later. Thank you. Oh . . . hold my calls until I tell you."

After she closed the door I just sat there and tried to collect my thoughts . . . chasing elusive and ephemeral butterflies of irrational images . . . trying to ignore the pain in my head . . . and in the pit of my stomach. Was I cracking up? Was this how a nervous breakdown climaxes in the frightening inability to connect one rational thought with another? Is this what all those executive seminars and books warn you will happen if you push your body and mind to their limits and beyond, while trying to compress several lives into one in your mad dash for success? Does the mind finally switch channels on you and

force you to participate in a fantasyland of acts and
conversations with characters dredged from some
long-forgotten childhood storybook? Is this the ultimate escape when pressures and responsibilities grow
too big to handle?

Was Simon just a dream? Impossible. Still, if Simon
was nearly always around the parking lot each morning why hadn't Pat ever seen him? And what about
his apartment? Was somebody playing some sort of
macabre joke on me? Yet, why had I never discussed
him with anyone? And what about all his lectures . . .
those priceless hours of inspiration and knowledge
and hope? And how about the ragpicker thing . . .
pulling dropouts from the human race off the junk
pile . . . showing people how to perform the greatest
miracle in the world . . . dear God, I couldn't have
made all that up in my wildest creative moments.

I snapped back to some semblance of sanity when
I suddenly realized that I had been turning the brown
envelope over and over in my hand. The brown envelope—my only link to the truth . . . my only link to
Simon . . . my proof that he really existed! I found
myself rubbing the package as if, like some genii's
lamp, my touch would cause the old man to reappear.
I relaxed a little. If he had sent the package then
I wasn't crazy. Simon existed!

"Simon, Simon . . . where the hell are you? Don't
do this to me. I don't deserve this from you!"

I must have been close to the edge of shock . . . as
I yelled toward three empty orange chairs that faced
me across my desk. Finally, I turned over the brown
envelope, ripped open the flap, reached in and removed several sheets of typewritten paper held together with a paper clip.

As I did so a small object rolled from the envelope
onto my desk. I picked it up . . . a tiny safety pin
attached to a small piece of white rag measuring approximately half an inch square.

I pushed the pin aside. Attached to the paper clip that held the pages was a letter to me in the same handwriting as the envelope.

The letter was undated. . . .

CHAPTER EIGHT

Dear Mr. Og,

I am ill prepared to deal with the specific and time-consuming legalities of drawing up a last will and testament. Let this letter suffice.

During the past year you have brought love, companionship, laughter, and good conversation, not to mention an immortal red geranium, into the life of an old ragpicker.

Ragpickers, by the very nature of their chosen profession, are not accustomed to being on the receiving end of life's finer gifts, nor is it wise to become too closely attached to those whom one desires to help. Still there are times when teachers must be taught, doctors must be cured, lawyers must be defended, comedians must be amused, and even ragpickers must be loved.

I know you have loved me, as I love you.

It is fitting and right, therefore, that I bequeath the enclosed master copy of 'The God Memorandum' to you, not only to fulfill my promise but also to bring to a culmination that long series of seemingly miraculous coincidences between your book's great salesman and myself.

Perhaps after you have benefited from much introspection and thought regarding our relationship, you will be able to put the past twelve months in their proper perspective and even come to the eventual conclusion that it was not as difficult a task for me to write a memorandum for God as it is for you to accept its existence.

Since I know you to be an impetuous man I am certain that long before you have reached this portion of my letter you have already sought me out, in vain, and are now tormented with grief and concern for my well-being. Fear not. Banish all worry from your mind. In the words of another ragpicker, I now ask you to grieve no more . . . for where I go you cannot follow me now, but one day you will.

Do not forget that we have a contract, you and I. 'The God Memorandum' is now in your possession and it is my desire that you share it, eventually, with the world, but only after you apply its principles to your own life, consonant with my instructions.

Remember that the most difficult tasks are consummated, not by a single explosive burst of energy or effort, but by consistent daily application of the best you have within you.

To change one's life for the better, to resurrect one's body and mind from living death, requires many positive steps, one in front of the other, with your sights always on your goal.

'The God Memorandum' is only your ticket to a new life. It will do nothing for you unless you open your mind and your heart to receive it. By itself it will move you not one inch in any direction. The means of transportation, and the power to break your inertia, must be generated by forces long dormant but still alive within you. Follow these rules and your forces will self-ignite:

1. First, mark this day upon your calendar. Then, count forward one hundred days and mark that day. This will establish the length of your mission without the necessity of your counting each day as you live it.

2. Next in this envelope you will find a small safety pin to which has been attached a tiny piece of white rag in the shape of a square. This combination of pin

and rag, two of the most common and unprepossess-
ing materials in the world, is your ragpicker's secret
amulet. Wear your amulet on your person in a place
visible to you as a constant reminder, during the next
hundred days, that you are trying to live as you are
being instructed to live in 'The God Memorandum.'
Your pin and rag are symbols . . . a sign that you are
in the process of changing your life from the pins and
rags of failure to the treasures of a new and better life.

3. Do not, under any conditions divulge the meaning of your amulet to those who may inquire during
your hundred-day mission.

4. Read 'The God Memorandum' before you retire,
each night, for one hundred nights . . . and then sleep
in peace, while the message you have read gradually seeps down into your deep mind that never sleeps.
Let no reason or excuse force you to forego the reading for even one night.

Gradually, as the days became weeks, you will notice great changes in yourself . . . as will those around
you. By the hundredth day . . . you will be a living
miracle . . . a new person . . . filled with beauty and
wonder and ambition and ability.

Then, and only then, find someone who, like your
old self, needs help. Give him two things: your ragpicker's secret amulet . . . and 'The God Memorandum.'

And one more thing give to him . . . as I have given
to you . . . love.

I have a vision wherein I can see thousands upon
thousands wearing our ragpicker's amulets. People
will encounter each other in the marketplace, on the
street, in their places of worship, in their public con-
veyances, in their schools, and on their job and they
will look upon each other's insignificant pin and rag
and smile at their brothers and sisters . . . for each
will know that the other is embarked on the same
mission, the same dream, with a common purpose . . .

to change their own life for the better and thus, joined together, change their world.

Still, I prophesy many difficult situations ahead for you, Mister Og. Should you eventually decide to make 'The God Memorandum' part of a future book you will inevitably be asked, by your publisher, to make promotional tours as you have in the past for your other books. How will you explain 'The God Memorandum' since it will be impossible for you to either produce or even prove that its creator, its author, ever existed? Severe challenges will be made on your integrity and perhaps your sanity by those who will refuse to believe your story if you recount it as we have experienced it. And who can blame them? It has not been so long since humans were crucified, beheaded, or burned for far less than you will be required to say in order to be absolutely truthful about me and the 'Memorandum.'

Nevertheless, I leave it in your care with complete faith that you will tend it as you would a beloved child. I know how much you enjoy a dare and so I dare you to use it, yourself. I dare you to publish it, and I dare you to share it with the world.

Once you said you had a premonition about me. As you read these words you know that we shall not see each other again for a long time. There will be no more hours together when we can sip our sherry in the peace and warmth of a loving friendship that knew no boundaries of time or space. And I leave you, for now, not with sadness but with satisfaction and joy that we came together and walked, arm in arm, through this brief moment of eternity. Who could ask for more?

Someday, when the world closes in on you, as it will from time to time, pour yourself a glass of sherry and think of your old ragpicker. My blessings are with you always, and my only injunction to you is that you continue with your writing no matter what circumstances befall you. You have much yet to say. The world needs you. The ragpickers need you. I need you.

One of my dear friends, Socrates, in his last moments, said, "The hour of my departure has arrived, and we go our ways . . . I to die, and you to live. Which is better, God only knows."

Mister Og, I know which is better.

To live . . . is better.

Live in happiness . . . everlasting peace.

With love,
Simon

I dropped his letter and stared at the pages of type.

I picked up the small safety pin with its wisp of white rag and pinned the amulet to my jacket lapel.

I reached across the desk and drew my five-year calendar toward me.

I circled the date and counted forward one hundred days, bringing me well into the new year.

I circled the hundredth day.

Tonight, before I turned off my bedside light I would read 'The God Memorandum' as he had instructed.

My hands were clenched together tightly. I lowered my head to my desk until my forehead touched it.

Why was I crying? Was it because Simon had left me? Was it because I had suspected, too late, his true identity? Or was it because I knew that my life, my dreams, my world, would never be the same again, now that he had placed his hand upon them. . . .

CHAPTER NINE

THE GOD MEMORANDUM

To: You
From: God

Take counsel.

I hear your cry.

It passes through the darkness, filters through the clouds, mingles with starlight, and finds its way to my heart on the path of a sunbeam.

I have anguished over the cry of a hare choked in the noose of a snare, a sparrow tumbled from the nest of its mother, a child thrashing helplessly in a pond, and a son shedding his blood on a cross.

Know that I hear you, also. Be at peace. Be calm.

I bring thee relief for your sorrow for I know its cause . . . and its cure.

You weep for all your childhood dreams that have vanished with the years.

You weep for all your self-esteem that has been corrupted by failure.

You weep for all your potential that has been bartered for security.

You weep for all your individuality that has been trampled by mobs.

You weep for all your talent that has been wasted through misuse.

You look upon yourself with disgrace and you turn in terror from the image you see in the pool. Who is this mockery of humanity staring back at you with bloodless eyes of shame?

Where is the grace of your manner, the beauty of your figure, the quickness of your movement, the clarity of your mind, the brilliance of your tongue? Who stole your goods? Is the thief's identity known to you, as it is to me?

Once you placed your head in a pillow of grass in your father's field and looked up at a cathedral of clouds and knew that all the gold of Babylon would be yours in time.

Once you read from many books and wrote on many tablets, convinced beyond any doubt that all the wisdom of Solomon would be equaled and surpassed by you.

And the seasons would flow into years until lo, you would reign supreme in your own garden of Eden.

Dost thou remember who implanted those plans and dreams and seeds of hope within you?

You cannot.

You have no memory of that moment when first you emerged from your mother's womb and I placed my hand on your soft brow. And the secret I whispered in your small ear when I bestowed my blessings upon you?

Remember our secret?

You cannot.

The passing years have destroyed your recollection, for they have filled your mind with fear and doubt and anxiety and remorse and hate and there is no room for joyful memories where these beasts habitate.

Weep no more. I am with you . . . and this moment is the dividing line of your life. All that has gone before is like unto no more than that time you slept within your mother's womb. What is past is dead. Let the dead bury the dead.

This day you return from the living dead.

This day, like unto Elijah with the widow's son, I stretch myself upon thee three times and you live again.

This day, like unto Elisha with the Shunammite's son, I put my mouth upon your mouth and my eyes upon your eyes and my hands upon your hands and your flesh is warm again.

This day, like unto Jesus at the tomb of Lazarus, I command you to come forth and you will walk from your cave of doom to begin a new life.

This is your birthday. This is your new date of birth. Your first life, like unto a play of the theatre, was only a rehearsal. This time the curtain is up. This time the world watches and waits to applaud. This time you will not fail.

Light your candles. Share your cake. Pour the wine. You have been reborn.

Like a butterfly from its chrysalis you will fly . . . fly as high as you wish, and neither the wasps nor dragonflies nor mantids of mankind shall obstruct your mission or your search for the true riches of life.

Feel my hand upon thy head.

Attend to my wisdom.

Let me share with you, again, the secret you heard at your birth and forgot.

You are my greatest miracle.

You are the greatest miracle in the world.

Those were the first words you ever heard. Then you cried. They all cry.

You did not believe me then . . . and nothing has happened in the intervening years to correct your disbelief. For how could you be a miracle when you consider yourself a failure at the most menial of tasks? How can you be a miracle when you have little confidence in dealing with the most trivial of responsibilities? How can you be a miracle when you are shackled by debt and lie awake in torment over whence will come tomorrow's bread?

Enough. The milk that is spilled is sour. Yet, how many prophets, how many wise men, how many poets, how many artists, how many composers, how many scientists, how many philosophers and messengers have I sent with word of your divinity, your potential for godliness, and the secrets of achievement? How did you treat them?

Still I love you and I am with you now, through these words, to fulfill the prophet who announced that the Lord shall set his hand again, the second time, to recover the remnant of his people.

I have set my hand again.

This is the second time.

You are my remnant.

It is of no avail to ask, haven't you known, haven't you heard, hasn't it been told to you from the beginning; haven't you understood from the foundations of the earth?

You have not known; you have not heard; you have not understood.

You have been told that you are a divinity in disguise, a god playing a fool.

You have been told that you are a special piece of work, noble in reason, infinite in faculties, express and admirable in form and moving, like an angel in action, like a god in apprehension.

You have been told that you are the salt of the earth.

You were given the secret even of moving mountains, of performing the impossible.

You believed no one. You burned your map to happiness, you abandoned your claim to peace of mind, you snuffed out the candles that had been placed along your destined path of glory, and then you stumbled, lost and frightened, in the darkness of futility and self-pity, until you fell into a hell of your own creation.

Then you cried and beat your breast and cursed the luck that had befallen you. You refused to accept

the consequences of your own petty thoughts and lazy
deeds and you searched for a scapegoat on which to
blame your failure. How quickly you found one.

You blamed me!

You cried that your handicaps, your mediocrity,
your lack of opportunity, your failures . . . were the
will of God!

You were wrong!

Let us take inventory. Let us, first, call a roll of
your handicaps. For how can I ask you to build a new
life lest you have the tools?

Are you blind? Does the sun rise and fall without
your witness?

No. You can see . . . and the hundred million
receptors I have placed in your eyes enable you to
enjoy the magic of a leaf, a snowflake, a pond, an
eagle, a child, a cloud, a star, a rose, a rainbow . . .
and the look of love. Count one blessing.

Are you deaf? Can a baby laugh or cry without
your attention?

No. You can hear . . . and the twenty-four thousand
fibers I have built in each of your ears vibrate to the
wind in the trees, the tides on the rocks, the majesty
of an opera, a robin's plea, children at play . . . and
the words I love you. Count another blessing.

Are you mute? Do your lips move and bring forth
only spittle?

No. You can speak . . . as can no other of my
creatures, and your words can calm the angry, up-
lift the despondent, goad the quitter, cheer the unhappy, warm the lonely, praise the worthy, encourage
the defeated, teach the ignorant . . . and say I love
you. Count another blessing.

Are you paralyzed? Does your helpless form despoil
the land?

No. You can move. You are not a tree condemned
to a small plot while the wind and world abuses you.
You can stretch and run and dance and work, for
within you I have designed five hundred muscles, two

hundred bones, and seven miles of nerve fibre all synchronized by me to do your bidding. Count another blessing.

Are you unloved and unloving? Does loneliness engulf you, night and day?

No. No more. For now you know love's secret, that to receive love it must be given with no thought of its return. To love for fulfillment, satisfaction, or pride is no love. Love is a gift on which no return is demanded. Now you know that to love unselfishly is its own reward. And even should love not be returned it is not lost, for love not reciprocated will flow back to you and soften and purify your heart. Count another blessing. Count twice.

Is your heart stricken? Does it leak and strain to maintain your life?

No. Your heart is strong. Touch your chest and feel its rhythm, pulsating, hour after hour, day and night, thirty-six million beats each year, year after year, asleep or awake, pumping your blood through more than sixty thousand miles of veins, arteries, and tubing . . . pumping more than six hundred thousand gallons each year. Man has never created such a machine. Count another blessing.

Are you diseased of skin? Do people turn in horror when you approach?

No. Your skin is clear and a marvel of creation, needing only that you tend it with soap and oil and brush and care. In time all steels will tarnish and rust, but not your skin. Eventually the strongest of metals will wear, with use, but not that layer that I have constructed around you. Constantly it renews itself, old cells replaced by new, just as the old you is now replaced by the new. Count another blessing.

Are your lungs befouled? Does the breath of life struggle to enter your body?

No. Your portholes to life support you even in the vilest of environments of your own making, and they labor always to filter life-giving oxygen through six hundred million pockets of folded flesh while they rid your body of gaseous wastes. Count another blessing.

Is your blood poisoned? Is it diluted with water and pus?

No. Within your five quarts of blood are twenty-two trillion blood cells and within each cell are millions of molecules and within each molecule is an atom oscillating at more than ten million times each second. Each second, two million of your blood cells die to be replaced by two million more in a resurrection that has continued since your first birth. As it has always been inside, so now it is on your outside. Count another blessing.

Are you feeble of mind? Can you no longer think for yourself?

No. Your brain is the most complex structure in the universe. I know. Within its three pounds are thirteen billion nerve cells, more than three times as many cells as there are people on your earth. To help you file away every perception, every sound, every taste, every smell, every action you have experienced since the day of your birth, I have implanted, within your cells, more than one thousand billion billion protein molecules. Every incident in your life is there waiting only your recall. And, to assist your brain in the control of your body I have dispersed, throughout your form, four million pain-sensitive structures, five hundred thousand touch detectors, and more than two hundred thousand temperature detectors. No nation's gold is better protected than you. None of your ancient wonders are greater than you.

You are my finest creation.

Within you is enough atomic energy to destroy any of the world's great cities . . . and rebuild it.

Are you poor? Is there no gold or silver in your purse?

No. You are rich! Together we have just counted your wealth. Study the list. Count them again. Tally your assets!

Why have you betrayed yourself? Why have you cried that all the blessings of humanity were removed from you? Why did you deceive yourself that you were powerless to change your life? Are you without talent, senses, abilities, pleasures, instincts, sensations, and pride? Are you without hope? Why do you cringe in the shadows, a giant defeated, awaiting only sympathetic transport into the welcome void and dampness of hell?

You have so much. Your blessings overflow your cup . . . and you have been unmindful of them, like a child spoiled in luxury, since I have bestowed them upon you with generosity and regularity.

Answer me.

Answer yourself.

What rich man, old and sick, feeble and helpless, would not exchange all the gold in his vault for the blessings you have treated so lightly.

Know then the first secret to happiness and success —that you possess, even now, every blessing necessary to achieve great glory. They are your treasure, your tools with which to build, starting today, the foundation for a new and better life.

Therefore, I say unto you, count your blessings and know that you already are my greatest creation. This is the first law you must obey in order to perform the greatest miracle in the world, the return of your humanity from living death.

And be grateful for your lessons learned in poverty. For he is not poor who has little; only he that desires much . . . and true security lies not in the things one has but in the things one can do without.

Where are the handicaps that produced your failure? They existed only in your mind.

Count your blessings.

And the second law is like unto the first. Proclaim your rarity.

You had condemned yourself to a potter's field, and there you lay, unable to forgive your own failure, destroying yourself with self-hate, self-incrimination, and revulsion at your crimes against yourself and others.

Are you not perplexed?

Do you not wonder why I am able to forgive your failures, your transgressions, your pitiful demeanor . . . when you cannot forgive yourself?

I address you now, for three reasons. You need me. You are not one of a herd heading for destruction in a gray mass of mediocrity. And . . . you are a great rarity.

Consider a painting by Rembrandt or a bronze by Degas or a violin by Stradivarius or a play by Shakespeare. They have great value for two reasons: their creators were masters and they are few in number. Yet there are more than one of each of these.

On that reasoning you are the most valuable treasure on the face of the earth, for you know who created you and there is only one of you.

Never, in all the seventy billion humans who have walked this planet since the beginning of time has there been anyone exactly like you.

Never, until the end of time, will there be another such as you.

You have shown no knowledge or appreciation of your uniqueness.

Yet, you are the rarest thing in the world.

From your father, in his moment of supreme love, flowed countless seeds of love, more than four hundred million in number. All of them, as they swam within your mother, gave up the ghost and died. All except one! You.

You alone persevered within the loving warmth of your mother's body, searching for your other half, a single cell from your mother so small that more than two million would be necessary to fill an acorn shell. Yet, despite impossible odds, in that vast ocean of darkness and disaster, you persevered, found that infinitesmal cell, joined with it, and began a new life. Your life.

You arrived, bringing with you, as does every child, the message that I was not yet discouraged of man. Two cells now united in a miracle. Two cells, each containing twenty-three chromosomes and within each chromosome hundreds of genes, which would govern every characteristic about you, from the color of your eyes to the charm of your manner, to the size of your brain.

With all the combinations at my command, beginning with that single sperm from your father's four hundred million, through the hundreds of genes in each of the chromosomes from your mother and father, I could have created three hundred thousand billion humans, each different from the other.

But who did I bring forth?

You! One of a kind. Rarest of the rare. A priceless treasure, possessed of qualities in mind and speech and movement and appearance and actions as no other who has ever lived, lives, or shall live.

Why have you valued yourself in pennies when you are worth a king's ransom?

Why did you listen to those who demeaned you ... and far worse, why did you believe them?

Take counsel. No longer hide your rarity in the dark. Bring it forth. Show the world. Strive not to walk as your brother walks, nor talk as your leader talks, nor labor as do the mediocre. Never do as another. Never imitate. For how do you know that you may not imitate evil; and he who imitates evil always goes beyond the example set, while he who imitates what is good always falls short. Imitate no one. Be yourself. Show your rarity to the world and they will shower you with gold. This then is the second law.

Proclaim your rarity.

And now you have received two laws.

Count your blessings! Proclaim your rarity!

You have no handicaps. You are not mediocre.

You nod. You force a smile. You admit your self-deception.

What of your next complaint? Opportunity never seeks thee?

Take counsel and it shall come to pass, for now I give you the law of success in every venture. Many centuries ago this law was given to your forefathers from a mountain top. Some heeded the law and lo, their life was filled with the fruit of happiness, accomplishment, gold, and peace of mind. Most listened not, for they sought magic means, devious routes, or waited for the devil called luck to deliver to them the riches of life. They waited in vain . . . just as you waited, and then they wept, as you wept, blaming their lack of fortune on my will.

The law is simple. Young or old, pauper or king, white or black, male or female . . . all can use the secret to their advantage; for of all the rules and speeches and scriptures of success and how to attain it, only one method has never failed . . . whomsoever shall compel ye to go with him one mile . . . go with him two.

This then is the third law . . . the secret that will produce riches and acclaim beyond your dreams. Go another mile!

The only certain means of success is to render more and better service than is expected of you, no matter what your task may be. This is a habit followed by all successful people since the beginning of time. Therefore I saith the surest way to doom yourself to mediocrity is to perform only the work for which you are paid.

Think not ye are being cheated if you deliver more than the silver you receive. For there is a pendulum to all life and the sweat you deliver, if not rewarded today, will swing back tomorrow, tenfold. The mediocre never goes another mile, for why should he cheat himself, he thinks. But you are not mediocre. To go another mile is a privilege you must appropriate by your own initiative. You cannot, you must not avoid it. Neglect it, do only as little as the others, and the responsibility for your failure is yours alone.

You can no more render service without receiving just compensation than you can withhold the rendering of it without suffering the loss of reward. Cause and effect, means and ends, seed and fruit, these cannot be separated. The effect already blooms in the cause, the end pre-exists in the means, and the fruit is always in the seed.

Go another mile.

Concern yourself not, should you serve an ungrateful master. Serve him more.

And instead of him, let it be me who is in your debt, for then you will know that every minute, every stroke of extra service will be repaid. And worry not, should your reward not come soon. For the longer payment is withheld, the better for you . . . and compound interest on compound interest is this law's greatest benefit.

You cannot command success, you can only deserve it . . . and now you know the great secret necessary in order to merit its rare reward.

Go another mile!

Where is this field whence you cried there was no opportunity? Look! Look around thee. See, where only yesterday you wallowed on the refuse of self-pity, you now walk tall on a carpet of gold. Nothing has changed . . . except you, but you are everything.

You are my greatest miracle.

You are the greatest miracle in the world.

And now the laws of happiness and success are three.

Count your blessings! Proclaim your rarity! Go another mile!

Be patient with your progress. To count your blessings with gratitude, to proclaim your rarity with pride, to go an extra mile and then another, these acts are not accomplished in the blinking of an eye. Yet, that which you acquire with most difficulty you retain the longest; as those who have earned a fortune are more careful of it than those by whom it was inherited.

And fear not as you enter your new life. Every noble acquisition is attended with its risks. He who fears to encounter the one must not expect to obtain the other. Now you know you are a miracle. And there is no fear in a miracle.

Be proud. You are not the momentary whim of a careless creator experimenting in the laboratory of life. You are not a slave of forces that you cannot comprehend. You are a free manifestation of no force but mine, of no love but mine. You were made with a purpose.

Feel my hand. Hear my words.

You need me . . . and I need you.

We have a world to rebuild . . . and if it requireth a miracle what is that to us? We are both miracles and now we have each other.

Never have I lost faith in you since that day when I first spun you from a giant wave and tossed you helplessly on the sands. As you measure time that was more than five hundred million years ago. There were many models, many shapes, many sizes, before I reached perfection in you more than thirty thousand years ago. I have made no further effort to improve on you in all these years.

For how could one improve on a miracle? You were a marvel to behold and I was pleased. I gave you this world and dominion over it. Then, to enable you to reach your full potential I placed my hand upon you, once more, and endowed you with powers unknown to any other creature in the universe, even unto this day.

I gave you the power to think.

I gave you the power to love.

I gave you the power to will.

I gave you the power to laugh.

I gave you the power to imagine.

I gave you the power to create.

I gave you the power to plan.

I gave you the power to speak.

I gave you the power to pray.

My pride in you knew no bounds. You were my ultimate creation, my greatest miracle. A complete living being. One who can adjust to any climate, any hardship, any challenge. One who can manage his own destiny without any interference from me. One who can translate a sensation or perception, not by instinct, but by thought and deliberation into whatever action is best for himself and all humanity.

Thus we come to the fourth law of success and happiness . . . for I gave you one more power, a power so great that not even my angels possess it.

I gave you . . . the power to choose.

With this gift I placed you even above my angels . . . for angels are not free to choose sin. I gave you complete control over your destiny. I told you to determine, for yourself, your own nature in accordance with your own free will. Neither heavenly nor earthly in nature, you were free to fashion yourself in whatever form you preferred. You had the power to choose to degenerate into the lowest forms of life, but you also had the power, out of your soul's judgment, to be reborn into the higher forms, which are divine.

I have never withdrawn your great power, the power to choose.

What have you done with this tremendous force? Look at yourself. Think of the choices you have made in your life and recall, now, those bitter moments when you would fall to your knees if only you had the opportunity to choose again.

What is past is past . . . and now you know the

fourth great law of happiness and success . . . Use wisely, your power of choice.

Choose to love . . . rather than hate.
Choose to laugh . . . rather than cry.
Choose to create . . . rather than destroy.
Choose to persevere . . . rather than quit.
Choose to praise . . . rather than gossip.
Choose to heal . . . rather than wound.
Choose to give . . . rather than steal.
Choose to act . . . rather than procrastinate.
Choose to grow . . . rather than rot.
Choose to pray . . . rather than curse.
Choose to live . . . rather than die.

Now you know that your misfortunes were not my will, for all power was vested in you, and the accumulation of deeds and thoughts which placed you on the refuse of humanity were your doing, not mine. My gifts of power were too large for your small nature. Now you have grown tall and wise and the fruits of the land will be yours.

You are more than a human being, you are a human becoming.

You are capable of great wonders. Your potential is unlimited. Who else, among my creatures, has mastered fire? Who else, among my creatures, has conquered gravity, has pierced the heavens, has conquered disease and pestilence and drought?

Never demean yourself again!
Never settle for the crumbs of life!
Never hide your talents, from this day hence!

Remember the child who says, "when I am a big boy." But what is that? For the big boy says, "when I grow up." And then grown up, he says, "when I am wed." But to be wed, what is that, after all? The thought then changes to "when I retire." And then, retirement comes, and he looks back over the landscape traversed; a cold wind sweeps over it and somehow he has missed it all and it is gone.

Enjoy this day, today . . . and tomorrow, tomorrow.

You have performed the greatest miracle in the world.

You have returned from a living death.

You will feel self-pity no more and each new day will be a challenge and a joy.

You have been born again . . . but just as before, you can choose failure and despair or success and happiness. The choice is yours. The choice is exclusively yours. I can only watch, as before . . . in pride . . . or sorrow.

Remember, then, the four laws of happiness and success.

- Count your blessings.
- Proclaim your rarity.
- Go another mile.
- Use wisely your power of choice.

And one more, to fulfill the other four. Do all things with love . . . love for yourself, love for all others, and love for me.)   LoVE WELL

Wipe away your tears. Reach out, grasp my hand, and stand straight.

Let me cut the grave cloths that have bound you.

This day you have been notified.

YOU ARE THE GREATEST MIRACLE IN THE WORLD

CHAPTER TEN

❉❉❉❉❉❉❉❉❉❉❉❉❉❉❉❉❉❉❉❉❉❉❉❉

I believe all office Christmas parties should be abolished! There's just no way to prevent at least one poor soul from trying to work off his or her pent-up repressions or holiday melancholia in a fit of drinking that either ends up in a scene that will be regretted later or climaxes in a fight over someone's right to get into an automobile and kill himself or some innocent soul. I know. I've acted the fool myself a couple of times . . . long ago.

Furthermore, that "cold duck" leaves permanent scars on office carpeting that no cleaning fluid has ever completely removed.

Each year I resolve, usually on the first work day following Christmas, that next year there will be no party in our office. We'll give that foolishly spent money to some needy-family fund instead. And each year, when committees begin to form to plan "the party," I weaken, plead "no contest," and allow it to happen again.

So . . . I had a couple of drinks and tried to smile through the silliness of the grab-bag exchange while someone's record player monotonously abused a scratchy version of "White Christmas." Then I walked around, patting shoulders and kissing cheeks, feeling like a house detective, constantly reassuring myself that everyone would make it home without any spontaneous motel stops or drunken-driving violations.

Finally the wine ran out and the office emptied swiftly, leaving in its wake a collection of debris that would only be removed if I left a twenty-dollar bill for our cleaning man. It was already in a Christmas card, propped up on Pat's desk where he wouldn't miss it.

I carried my last glass of wine into my office and fell wearily onto the couch, setting the glass into a standing ash tray. The glass. I found myself staring at it, almost hypnotized. Simon. All those sherry glasses we filled and emptied together. Simon. Simon. Where are you?

Suddenly I reached a decision and went to my desk. I punched "F" on my telephone index gadget and found Fred Fell's home phone number. I dialed it. He recognized my voice as soon as I said, "Happy Holidays."

"Og, how wonderful to hear from you. How are you? How's the weather in Chicago?"

"We've got snow."

"Here it's been raining for two days. I think Long Island is sinking."

"So head for Miami."

"I think it's too late. What's going on with you?"

"We've just had our Christmas party in the office ..."

". . . and you've had a few drinks and got a little sentimental and remembered your old publisher?"

"All that . . . and one more reason."

"Tell me."

"I'm ready to do another book."

"I don't believe what I'm hearing. I was beginning to think you were so busy counting your money and making like Gore Vidal on all those talk shows that there was no time for writing, anymore. What do you want to do? What's the book about?"

"I'm not going to tell you. There's no way I can explain it, either on the phone or in person. I'm just going to do it."

"Does it have a title?"

"*The Greatest Miracle In The World.*"

"I like it already. What's the big miracle?"

"Don't ask."

"Will it be another like *The Greatest Salesman In The World*?"

"Better. I don't have to make this one up."

"Okay, Og. I know better than to push you. You want a contract?"

"No hurry. Whenever you get around to it."

"Same terms as before?"

"Fine."

"What should I put down for delivery date of manuscript?"

"Make it . . . January thirty-first, nineteen-seventy-five."

"That's a year and a month from now. You need that long?"

"Yes."

"Very well. Consider it done. What a relationship we have! I wonder how many other publishers contract for books like this, without even knowing what they're buying?"

"Mailer's publisher, Wallace's publisher, Updike's publisher, Fowles' publisher, Michener's publisher, Herriot's publisher . . ."

"Merry Christmas, Og."

"You too, Fred. Love you."

"I love you, too."

It was very dark and still snowing when I left the office and laid down a row of footprints all the way to the parking lot. I felt a burning emptiness inside me and I knew why. Across the lot I could see the dark shadows of the apartment where I had spent so many happy hours, its silent hulk checkered here and there with squares of light blinking through the falling snow.

Right about now we'd be wishing each other "Merry Christmas" and touching glasses and his beautiful voice would be washing over me as he opened whatever silly gift I would have brought. Simon. Simon.

"I miss you. I miss you very much." I was speaking aloud . . . to the wind and the snow flakes. Then I was fighting back sobs that seemed to start deep in my gut. I felt absolutely alone . . . and lost.

Finally I forced myself to shape up. I had to get home. There was still some shopping to do. Life does go on.

I fumbled for the car keys and unlocked the door. As I turned the key in the ignition I had the sudden compelling urge for another drink. But I knew what would happen: one would lead to twenty . . . and no matter in how many bars I looked I wouldn't find Simon.

I backed the car and cut it sharply toward the exit gate, its tires crunching noisily on the newly fallen snow. I rolled down my window and reached out to turn my key in the gate-release slot. The gate creaked and rose slowly toward the sky. I shifted into "drive" and accelerated slowly over the small asphalt mound under the gate. The front of my car pointed upward slightly as it reached the crest of the mound and the headlight beams swept across a second-floor-apartment window that was dark.

I blinked my eyes and shook my head. I looked again.

My headlight beams had converged in a single shaft of light on a window box.

My God!

In the box was a plant—tilting gently in the blowing snow . . .

. . . A beautiful plant!

. . . A blue-ribbon plant!

. . . A red glass geranium.

A special preview of Og Mandino's

THE GREATEST SALESMAN IN THE WORLD PART II
The End of the Story

On the outskirts of Damascus, in a stately palace of burnished marble framed by giant palm trees, there lived a very special man whose name was Hafid. Now retired, his vast trade empire had once known no boundaries, extending across so many lands from Parthia to Rome to Britannia that he was acclaimed everywhere as the greatest salesman in the world.

By the time he had removed himself from the world of commerce, following his twenty-sixth year of record growth and profit, the inspiring story of Hafid's rise from a lowly camel boy to his mighty position of power and wealth had spread throughout the civilized world.

In those times of great turmoil and upheaval, while almost all of the civilized world bowed meekly to Caesar and his armies, Hafid's fame and reputation had almost elevated him to the status of a living legend. Especially among the poor and downtrodden of Palestine, a border region on the eastern frontier of the empire, Hafid of Damascus was honored in song and poetry as a shining example of how much it was possible to accomplish with one's life despite obstacles and handicaps.

And yet, for a man who had fashioned such a monumental legacy and accumulated a fortune of several million gold talents, the greatest salesman in the world was far from happy in his retirement.

As he had done on so many other days stretching back through the years, Hafid emerged from the rear entrance of his mansion at dawn one morning, treading carefully on the dew-moistened tiles of polished basalt as he headed resolutely across the huge and shadowy courtyard. Far off, a solitary cock crowed as the sun's first rays of silver and gold radiated above the desert from the east.

Hafid paused near the octagonal fountain in the center of the wide patio and inhaled deeply, nodding in appreciation at the thick covering of pale yellow jasmine blossoms clinging to the high stone walls that surrounded his estate. He tightened the girdle of leather at his waist, tugged at his soft linen tunic, and continued at a slower pace until he had passed beneath a natural arcade of cypress boughs and was standing before an elevated granite tomb that was free of all ornamentation.

"Good morning, my beloved Lisha," he half-whispered, reaching forward and softly caressing a white rosebud extending from a single tall bush that guarded the vault's heavy bronze door. Then he retreated to his nearby bench of carved mahogany and sat staring at the crypt that contained the remains of the loving woman who had shared his life, his struggles, and his triumphs.

Hafid felt the pressure of a hand on his shoulder and heard the familiar and hoarse voice of his longtime bookkeeper and faithful companion, Erasmus, even before he opened his eyes.

"Forgive me, master . . . "

"Good morning, old friend."

Erasmus smiled, pointing up at the sun that was now directly above their heads. "Morning has already departed, master. Good afternoon."

Hafid sighed and shook his head. "Another peril of old age. One never sleeps at night, always arises before dawn, and then slumbers like a kitten through the entire day. There is no logic to that. None."

Erasmus nodded and folded his arms, expecting to hear another lecture on the sorrows of growing old. But this was not to be like every other morning, for Hafid had suddenly leaped to his feet and raced toward the tomb in long strides until his hand was on the stone. Then he turned and in a strong voice exclaimed, "I have become a sorry excuse for a human being! Tell me, Erasmus, how long has it been, now, since I began this selfish and isolated life devoted only to feeling sorry for myself?"

Erasmus stared wide-eyed and then replied, "The great change in thee commenced with the passing of Lisha and your sudden decision to dispose of all your emporiums and caravans, following her entombment. Fourteen years have run their course since you decided to turn your back on the world."

Hafid's eyes had become moist. "Precious ally and brother, how have you managed to tolerate my miserable behavior for so long?"

The old bookkeeper stared down at his hands. "We have been together for almost forty years and my love for you is unconditional. I served you during your greatest moments of success and happiness and I serve you now, just as willingly, even though I have agonized at the living death you seem to have willed for yourself. You cannot return Lisha to life and so you have been trying to join her in that tomb. Remember when you instructed me, many years ago, to secure a red rosebush and plant it next to this white one, after you were dead and laid to rest there?"

"Yes," replied Hafid, "and let us not forget my constant reminders that this palace and warehouse would be yours upon my death. A small recompense for your countless years of loyalty and friendship and all that you have endured from me since we lost Lisha."

Hafid reached out, snapped the stem of the solitary white rosebud, and carried it back to the bench where he placed it carefully in his old friend's lap. "Self-pity is the most terrible of diseases, Erasmus, and I have been afflicted far too long. I have foolishly divorced myself from all humanity, because of my great grief, and made myself a hermit in that mausoleum where you and I reside. Enough! It is time for change!"

"But they have not been wasted years, master.

Thy great charitable contributions to the underprivileged of Damascus . . . "

Hafid interrupted. "Money? What sacrifice was that for me? All people of wealth salve their conscience with gifts of gold for the poor. The rich feed off these contributions as much as the hungry and they make certain that the world is made aware of their great generosity which, to them, is no more than a handful of pennies. No, dear friend, applaud not my charity. Instead, sympathize with my unwillingness to share more of myself. . . . "

"And yet," protested Erasmus, "thy seclusion accomplished some good, sire. Have ye not filled thy library with the works of the world's great minds and devoted countless hours to the study of their ideas and principles?"

Hafid nodded. "I have made every attempt to occupy the long days and nights by giving myself the education I never received as a youth and the effort has opened my eyes to a world of wonder and promise that I had little time to appreciate in my pursuit after gold and success. Still, I have prolonged my grief far too long. This world has provided me with everything a man could desire. It is time I began to repay my debt by doing all I can to help make a better life for all mankind. I am not yet ready for my final resting place and the red rose I instructed that you plant here, upon my death, next to this white one that was Lisha's favorite, must wait."

Tears of joy were now flowing down the wrinkled cheeks of Erasmus as Hafid continued. "Livy was writing his history of Rome when he was seventy-five and Tiberius ruled the empire until almost eighty. Compared to them I am only a child . . . a healthy child of sixty! My lungs are clear, my flesh is firm, my vision is excellent, my heart is strong, and my mind is as alert as it was at twenty. I believe I am prepared for a second life . . . !"

"This is such a great miracle!" Erasmus cried, looking toward the heavens. "After years of silent anguish and grief over thy condition, my prayers have finally been answered. Tell me, sire, what has caused this surprise resurrection of the man who was so loved and respected by the world?"

Hafid smiled.